Y0-BRR-772

CHILD WELFARE LEAGUE OF AMERICA

STANDARDS FOR RESIDENTIAL CENTERS FOR CHILDREN

Child Welfare League of America, Inc.
440 First Street, NW, Suite 310, Washington, DC 20001-2085

WITHDRAWN
St. Scholastica Library
Duluth, Minnesota 55811

HV
741
.C5345
1982

Copyright © 1982 by the Child Welfare League of America, Inc.

ALL RIGHTS RESERVED.

Neither this book nor any part may be reproduced or transmitted in any form or by any means, electronic or mechanical, including photocopying, microfilming, and recording, or by any information storage and retrieval system, without permission in writing from the publisher.

CHILD WELFARE LEAGUE OF AMERICA, INC.

67 Irving Place, New York, NY 10003

Current printing (last digit)
10 9 8 7 6 5 4 3 2

PRINTED IN THE UNITED STATES OF AMERICA

Library of Congress Cataloging in Publication Data

Child Welfare League of America.
    Child Welfare League of America standards
    for residential centers for children.

    1. Children—Services for—Standards—
    United States.   2. Child Welfare League of
    America.   I. Title.
HV741.C5345   1982a   362.7'32'0218   82-4237
ISBN 0-87868-179-5   AACR2

ACKNOWLEDGMENTS

These standards represent the work of the Technical Committee on Revision of CWLA Standards for Services of Child Welfare Institutions; the views of affiliates, state and provincial departments, League staff, and consultants; and the members of the Board of CWLA, who reviewed and approved the Standards for Residential Centers for Children.

The Technical Committee was chosen on the basis of its members' expert knowledge and was drawn from social agencies and national organizations concerned with services for children who require residential care. The committee's preliminary draft was submitted for comments from the groups mentioned.

A member of the original committee that formulated the earlier standards, Dr. Henry W. Maier, University of Washington, also made an analysis of the draft and submitted recommendations.

TECHNICAL COMMITTEE FOR STANDARDS FOR RESIDENTIAL CENTERS FOR CHILDREN

Chairman: Tommy Perkins, Community Services of Greater Chattanooga, Inc., Chattanooga
Eugene Baker, Ph.D., The Children's Village, Dobbs Ferry, New York
Jerome Beeker, Center for Youth Development and Research, St. Paul
Mel Collins, Child Welfare League of America, Inc., New York
John Carswell, Parsons Child and Family Center, Albany
Arthur W. Elrey, Jr., Arizona Children's Home Association, Tucson
*H. Wayne Hanna, Youth Horizons, Montreal
Ralph S. Lehman, Edgewood Children's Center, Webster Grove, Missouri
Winston J. Miller, Missouri Hill School for Boys, St. Louis
Larry Miesner, Michigan Department of Social Services, Lansing
*Eloise Moreland, Black Administrators in Child Welfare
*John K. Morton, Nebraska Center for Children and Youth, Lincoln
Arlin E. Ness, Starr Commonwealth for Boys, Albion, Michigan
John Petten, The Cleveland Christian Home, Inc., Cleveland
Jack Phelan, National Organization of Child Care Worker Associations, Inc.
S. Norman Sherry, M.D., American Academy of Pediatrics
*Don W. Strauss, Runaway House, Memphis
Gene L. Svebakken, Lutheran Child and Family Services, River Forest, Illinois
Jack Terpstra, Children's Bureau, Administration for Children, Youth, and Families, Department of Health and Human Resources
Robert Whitefield, United Methodist Youthville, Inc., Newton, Kansas
Staff: *Gloria T. Chevers, Standards Development, CWLA

---

* Affiliation when the standards were prepared.

COMMITTEE ON STANDARDS 1982
BOARD OF DIRECTORS, CHILD WELFARE LEAGUE OF AMERICA

*Chairwoman: Mrs. Lawrence A. Schei, Sacramento
*Lyman H. Black, Jr., Seattle
Mrs. James M. Cox, Midwest City, Oklahoma
Peter W. Forsythe, New York
Mrs. Paul-Marcel Gelinas, Montreal
Mrs. Wetonah Jones, Philadelphia
*Albert J. Morris, Brighton, Michigan
*Mrs. Michael F. Orr, New York
Mrs. James M. Sibley, Atlanta
*Mrs. Fred B. Smales, Kenoche, Hawaii

---

* Affiliation when the standards were prepared.

CONTENTS

FOREWORD

Setting standards and improving practice in all social services for children have been major functions of the Child Welfare League of America since its formation more than 60 years ago. The 1955 study of the League's function and program reaffirmed that:

> Continued development of standards designed to be used as objectives or goals, based on tested knowledge and approved practice in the various fields of service, should be given high priority in the League's program.

Standards point up assumptions that must be tested and offer clues for research to obtain the knowledge required to serve children better. As we come to know the essentials for healthy growth of all children, we must restate the responsibility of society that child welfare services discharge: to provide for the child who would otherwise lack the conditions and opportunities favorable to the development, use, and enjoyment of his or her individual capacities.

In 1955, the League undertook to formulate a series of standards for child welfare services in light of what is known today about the development of children, and tested, effective ways of serving them.

Standards for Services of Child Welfare Institutions was first published in 1964. *Standards for Residential Centers for Children* is in part a revision of the 1964 standards, but in addition to reflecting today's practice and knowledge in residential care, they have been developed as the foundation for a series of standards on residential services for children with specialized needs.

These standards were developed with the help of a technical committee with expert knowledge in this area of child welfare practice. They have also been critically reviewed by affiliated agencies with residential services, state departments of welfare, other organizations interested in this kind of care for children, and the Child Welfare League Board and staff. The final draft took into account all these critiques.

No standards of practice can be considered final; in one sense, the moment they are promulgated they are out of date. Standards must be subject to continual review and revision, in view of the constantly growing knowledge about children, human behavior, and human ills. Developments in social and medical sciences, policies, and programs, and shifting patterns of social values and social organization should be conducive to change in child welfare practice.

Edwin F. Watson
Executive Director, CWLA

HOW TO USE CWLA STANDARDS

CWLA Standards are designed so that readers can easily and quickly obtain needed information.

The table of contents provides a rapid review of the general areas covered.

For specific information on a particular practice, the index lists, in alphabetical order, each subject of interest and related categories in the text. Each standard is designated by a number. The digit before the decimal indicates the chapter where the standard can be found; the digits after the decimal designate its numerical order within the chapter. (Note that the number for the Introduction is 0.)

In many instances, the standard in the text is followed by discussion that provides the reader with rationale, principles, implications, or steps in carrying out the practice.

When various aspects of a standard are discussed in more than one standard, cross-references are noted, in parentheses, to other standards associated with, or part of the practice necessary for desirable service.

INTRODUCTION

These standards pertain to the care of children whose needs cannot be met in their own families or in foster families and who can benefit by the experiences and help that residential services can offer them and their families. Although the term "residential" refers to any domicile, it is used here to represent only group care, in contradistinction to family care.

The last three or four decades have been marked by a number of developments affecting residential services for children. In the absence of systematic data, most policies and practice decisions are still based primarily on value judgments and assumptions. These standards are thus based on past and present experiences, with recognition that greater agreement than now exists is needed to resolve some of the issues in the field.

In recent years, there has been a growing trend to specialized residential settings with staffing and facilities to meet the needs of groups of children with common problems and needs. Specialization has also stimulated a trend toward smaller facilities and shorter periods of residence.

In recognition of these developments, these standards for residential services were prepared to cover the basic philosophy and concepts common to all residential facilities. The basic principles of care and protection of the children and the services for them and their parents are true for all residential services. These would include administration, management, facilities, funding, principles of staffing, relationships with parents, community supports, etc.

Differential supplementary standards applicable to specialized services for children with particular needs, such as residential treatment for emotionally disturbed children, care for developmentally disabled children, care for runaways or other children needing temporary or emergency care are anticipated. The *CWLA Standards for Group Home Service for Children* was published in 1978.

CWLA standards serve as a stimulus and a goal for improving existing

1

services. The standards set down those practices that, at the present time, are considered desirable in providing a constructive service for individual children and their families. The practices are based on the best available knowledge and experience in social work and in related professional and scientific fields.

0.1 The residential center as a child welfare service

These standards apply to residential services provided by residential centers as a child welfare service by a social agency, supported by voluntary contributions or tax funds, under sectarian or nonsectarian auspices. Like other child welfare services, residential services are an expression of society's concern for children. They discharge a delegated responsibility that society is prepared to assume for children when parents are unable to carry their child rearing responsibility or need some assistance to do so. (1.1–1.11, 2–2.26)

> The use of residential centers may be due to difficulties in the family situation, problems of the child, or a lack of suitable resources in the community that prevents the child from having the care or treatment he or she requires while living at home or in the community in a foster home or a group home. (1.3, 1.5)
>
> Residential services require provision for the care and protection of the child, and for treatment of the specific social and psychological problems of the child that give rise to the need for the particular service or are associated with its selection. Residential services necessarily involve working with parents as an integral part of the service to the child and require interagency and community planning and cooperation. As a total service for the child and the family, residential centers use knowledge and skills developed in a variety of fields, particularly child care, child development, education, medicine, psychiatry, law, psychology, recreation, and social work. Social work is the professional field that carries primary responsibility for providing a child welfare service.

0.2 Common elements in residential care

Group care of children is provided in a variety of facilities with different purposes under social work, correctional, educational, medical, and religious auspices. There are residential facilities for dependent and neglected children, children with emotional and behavioral problems, children needing emergency or temporary care, physically handicapped children, developmentally disabled children, and mentally ill children.

Regardless of auspice, all residential care of children has child welfare aspects. The residential center assumes a degree of responsibility for providing conditions favorable to the growth and development of children who are not being reared for a time by their families, and for helping children and their parents with difficulties preventing the children from growing up in a family and enjoying the opportunities that, in our society, the family is primarily expected to provide.

A social agency that assumes this responsibility for a given group of children as one of its functions is administering a child welfare service. As residential services begin to develop programs based on knowledge of child development and treatment of social and psychological problems, it becomes increasingly difficult to distinguish among the services for children ordinarily classified as dependent, neglected, delinquent, or emotionally disturbed.

Regardless of setting, certain basic principles apply to all residential facilities serving children and, in fact, even to hospitals, or to boarding schools when used for foster care: separation of children from their families, care of children living in groups, planning of the daily group living program, treatment of social, behavioral, and emotional problems of children and parents. All residential care of children has certain core components that can be used differentially according to the needs and problems of individual children. (1.6)

The children accepted for care or treatment, their age, the nature of their problems, and the primary purpose and responsibility of the residential facility determine modifications of the daily living program, grouping of children, procedures, staffing, medical and educational provisions, and physical facilities.

Indian children who live in Indian schools to obtain their education are a special concern. Child welfare services for them and their families should be provided in addition to the educational services.

0.3 Selective use of residential care

Group care in residential facilities is one of the oldest and most elementary forms of care for children who cannot be cared for by their own families. Because of lack of development or deficiencies of other community services, there are many residential facilities that continue to be used for children for whom another type of care would be more suitable.

These standards are concerned with the selective use of residential centers that provide service and care for those children for whom they have a unique value. A careful study of the individual characteristics, problems, and family situation of each child and his or her family should determine a residential center that is the best choice of service. Refinement of the criteria for deciding which children should be accepted is still needed. (0.11, 1.5, 1.6).

Residential centers are expected to modify and adapt their program to provide what is needed by the children whom they accept and to help develop other appropriate forms of care, service, and treatment in the community for children who do not need residential care.

Distinct Values of Residential Care

Certain attributes of residential care have values that are not found in other types of care, and that distinguish it from other services. These attributes can be used differentially according to the particular needs and problems of children at a given time or under given circumstances, and have to be taken into consideration in selecting and planning residential care for a given child.

0.4 Group living experiences

Care in a residential center involves the child in a variety of groups and group living situations. A rich and stimulating group living program offers opportunities that the child can use selectively for a wide range of experiences, in activities, in relationships with other children and adults, and in a variety of groups. (3.2)

Both educational and therapeutic factors are inherent in group living experiences. The different forms of group experience, and the interaction with other children and adults, can be used as enriching and, when indicated, as remedial experiences in the care and treatment of the child.

0.5 Planning and integration

Since children in the residential center are in continuous 24-hour care, it is possible to plan the day-by-day living experiences of each child and to integrate these with a variety of intensive services in a way that will result in a harmonious approach to the child and that will stimulate improvement in his or her psychological and social functioning. (1.9)

The program for each child can be purposefully planned to help him or her develop competence in dealing with life situations and to learn to take responsibility for his or her own behavior through:

- developing skills
- experiencing success
- discovering creative abilities
- learning routines of living
- learning acceptable social behavior: habits, standards, manners, social usages, and the reasons for them
- finding out what is involved in living together with others
- relating to peers and adults
- having demands made on him or her and meeting social expectations appropriate to age and development
- having pleasurable experiences, e.g., celebrations for holidays, birthdays, special achievements
- having fun and enjoyment from everyday happenings that generate feelings of encouragement and confidence

The roles of the child care worker, social worker, physician, nurse, psychiatrist, psychologist, teacher, chaplain, and other staff members can be coordinated and integrated with the child's daily living experiences.

0.6 Favorable climate

Through its staff, program, and physical facilities, a residential facility can create an atmosphere that is favorable to children. (1.11)

Children can be encouraged to feel that:

- they are respected and understood as individuals
- people care about them and will take care of them
- they have a safe place where they can stay
- adults can help them deal with unacceptable behavior without being punitive, retaliatory, or rejecting
- they can receive protection and guidance in controlling their impulses until their own controls are established
- they have help with their problems in the group, at school, in the community, and with their families
- they have help to work with them toward their goals

Inservice training, supervision, and consultation are used to help all staff members develop the requisite skills.

0.7 Routines and controls

The routines and regulations required when a number of persons live together create a sense of continuity, regularity, and stability, and provide a framework that can simplify living for the confused child. (3.15, 3.16)

The daily program can be planned so that it is comfortably relaxed, appropriately stimulating, flexible, and yet balanced with sufficient routine and controls.

Children can know what to expect and on what to depend. When they participate in making some of the rules that govern the way they live, the setting of limits and expectations leads to self-control that can be helpful in the current situation and in later life; or in choosing whether or not to conform, the child learns about reasonable expectations and logical consequences.

0.8 Peer groups

The experience of being part of a peer group can help the child build social and personal strengths and experience group accomplishments.

The group offers opportunities to:
• form relationships easily without having to seek them out
• find acceptance and status in a group
• feel his or her part in contributing to the whole
• develop sensitivity and helpfulness to others
• take part in group decisions
• learn positive group values and standards of behavior
• accept routines and a way of life to which the group agrees
• identify with the group
• develop a feeling of being needed
• develop his or her own identity through testing out attitudes, roles, and kinds of behavior

The peer group allows for a balance between participation in groups and solitary occupations, between demands to maintain relationships with other children or adults and being left alone. The child may select one, two, or more peers as friends.

Group pressures from peers can serve to control excessive emotional demands of children on an adult or on each other.

The group situation makes it easier for some children, because of the desire to be like others, to conform to what is expected of them as members of the group rather than what is expected of them individually.

The variety of groups in a residential center allows for experimentation with new relationships, behaviors, positive and negative reactions, social skills, and acceptance of responsibility.

Many children, and especially adolescents, use the support of their peers to speak about or act out their problems while they strive for better ways to function. The group situation encourages them to move out of their shell, as they see others "in the same boat."

0.9 Relationships with adults

The residential center offers a variety of interpersonal relationships with different staff members, with relative freedom from the emotional demands and expectations inherent in family living and in the community. (0.6)

The child has a choice of adults to whom he or she can relate, and select models for what he or she would like to be.

At a given time, the child may have diluted relationships or a close relationship with only one adult, according to a personal inclination or treatment plan.

The child can learn at his or her own pace to trust and to feel esteemed.

The experience of being liked by adults can eventually give a child a sense of belonging without threat of total loss through desertion by any one person.

When necessary, adults can reach out to the child who stays apart so that the child is not left on an emotional island. The range and variety of experiences—not only the individual relationship with a therapist, child care worker, or teacher—can be used in ways that help the child identify and modify problems and build on existing strengths.

The understanding and skills that staff members develop through training and experience help them to temper and to time the affection they give the child, to find pleasure in the child's slow growth and change, and to cope more readily with irritating and out-of-the-ordinary behavior.

Staff members of a residential center, more than members of a family, are expected to have outside sources of personal satisfaction and enrichment, so that they do not depend entirely on the children and other staff members to meet their own emotional needs; thus, they are likely to make fewer personal demands upon the child than the child's family or foster family.

0.10 Tolerance of deviant behavior

Staff members can be helped to tolerate unusual behavior and expressions of hostility.

> Deviant behavior and angry feelings usually occur in the course of helping a child with serious difficulties.

> Physical and psychological proximity of a variety of staff members facilitates their work with the child and family. In particular, the child care worker and the social worker can share their problems and goals, and observe and understand better what is taking place. The adults can help the child and family become aware of their own feelings and behavior and assist them to change behavior that is not constructive.

0.11 Minimizing hazards in group living

Certain characteristics of group living constitute possible hazards for certain children. Some of these characteristics may have to be minimized or countered in planning the daily activities of a particular child.

> These characteristics present considerable variability:
> * individualization
> * personal attention
> * privacy of personal space
> * feeling of belonging
> * a large number of nonrelated children and adults
> * sharing with many other children and competing for adult attention
> * overstimulation or understimulation
> * availability of experiences children need
> * opportunities to make decisions and to learn to take responsibility
> * possibilities for individual choices
> * conformity to rules and routines where a large number of people live together

Changing Patterns in Residential Care

> Changes are occurring in social conditions, in characteristics of children requiring care away from their own homes, in concepts regarding the responsibility of society for children and their families, in knowledge about child development, and in modification and treatment of social and personal problems.

0.12 The changing role of residential centers for children and youth

Residential placement is no longer viewed as an end in itself. Permanence for the child has moved to the forefront as a central theme in program planning, administration, and supervision of all placement services.

The use of child care facilities is being reappraised because of renewed conviction about the distinctive values of living at home in the community.* It is clear, nevertheless, that some children will need a sheltered environment where well trained and experienced staff members plan and provide a program.

There is strong conviction that residential settings should be used only for children requiring specialized care. Many believe that the residential center no longer best serves the purpose it had in the past—rearing dependent children placed because of the death or disability of parents, financial need, or family breakdown. Many children in residential centers are reported to have a range of serious developmental and emotional problems similar to those children placed in residential facilities primarily for the purpose of treatment. Today, residential centers are faced with adapting their purposes and resources to carrying out a dual responsibility for which they are uniquely suited—care and treatment.

Planning and development of services in residential centers and in communities are increasingly influenced by the treatment needs of children with varying kinds of personal and social difficulties that affect their capacity to form close relationships, to control their impulses, to deal with reality, and, therefore, to benefit from family life experiences.

Demands have also been increasing for reliance on community-based services for children who are mentally retarded or those who have other developmental disabilities. Residential care is still needed for seriously retarded children, children with multiple handicaps that limit their functioning, and children and youths who need intensive service at times to foster further development.

0.13 Changing needs of children entering residential facilities

An increasing number of children are recognized to be in need of

---

* The 1970 census reported that about 44,000 children were living in group settings for dependent and neglected children. Earlier census reports indicated that in 1960, 70,725 children were in group settings for dependent and neglected children, and in 1950, about 95,000 children. More recent figures are unavailable but there is no evidence that the trend has changed.

treatment because of emotional and behavioral difficulties disruptive to life in a family or community. Moreover, recent redefinition in the juvenile justice system of the status of certain behaviors has resulted in the diversion of a sizable number of children to the child welfare system. Some of these children pose problems for social service agencies. Special skills are required to work with acting-out older children, and special facilities may be needed to provide appropriate care and treatment for them.

0.14 Treatment

A wide diversity of services and programs in residential facilities reflects differences in concepts of treatment, and in theories about the varied use of the elements of residential facilities that could be significant in bringing about a desired change in the condition or situation of a particular child or family. Major differences of opinion center on the following features.

Concepts of the program:

- as a group living experience designed to resolve a problem utilizing all components of the environment and all circumstances that affect the child
- as a clinical service provided by staff with professional education for direct help to the child or parents with medical, psychiatric, or psychological problems (through medical care, individual counseling, casework, groupwork, remedial education, psychotherapy)
- as a clinical service supplemented by planned daily group living

Focus:

- utilization of intact, healthy aspects of a child's functioning for learning and socialization
- exploration and modification of psychological problems and disorders

Therapeutic elements:

- a safe environment
- use of group processes
- use of relationships
- behavior modification techniques
- psychotherapy (individual, group, family)

Goals of treatment of child and family:

- achievement and integration of skills
- changes in behavior for community and family living
- overcoming fear and distrust in relationships
- realization of potentials as a person
- reorganization of personality

0.15 Living in small groups

Small living units of the cottage type are preferable to the congregate residential center because they offer greater possibilities for individualization, stimulation, and participation.

0.16 Group relations in the residential center

Recognition that group experiences are unique elements in growth has led to increasing use of groups for therapeutic purposes. Group experiences must be adapted, to the extent possible, to the needs of the child.

Much has been learned recently of the importance of interaction among children and adults, the effect of the group on feelings and behavior of children, and the use of planned group experiences.

Social groupworkers in a residential facility can apply their knowledge and skills in the group living setting and in the treatment programs for children.

0.17 Social work in residential centers

Social work services for children and their families are an essential part of residential services, beginning with intake and continuing throughout placement, discharge, and aftercare.

0.18 Child care work in residential centers

Child care workers in their daily care and living with children are directly responsible for strengthening the children's competence.

The need for specialized training for child care workers is recognized. Agencies themselves provide opportunities, through inservice training and supervision, for development of the knowledge, skills, and values required of staff who care for children who need therapeutic group care.

Specialized training in child care work is increasingly being offered in settings such as community colleges, universities, etc.

Basic Assumptions in Providing Residential Services

The following principles and values should be the basis for providing residential services.

0.19 Value of the individual

Any child, regardless of age, sex, race, color, creed, social circumstances, national or religious origin, or handicap, has the right to be respected as an individual and to have the best possible care in accordance with his or her needs.

0.20 Value of family life

In our culture, family life generally offers the best opportunities for meeting the normal developmental and socialization needs of children.

> All children need the affection and security of a family of which they feel they are a part.

> Any child who can live in a family and benefit by it should have the opportunity to do so.

0.21 Preservation of the family

It is best for children to be reared in their own families so long as it can meet their needs or help to do so.

> Services to enable parents to carry or resume their responsibilities to the best of their ability should be available in every community. These should include counseling, financial assistance, day care, day treatment, child protection, parent education, homemaker services, and other social and community services for children and their families in their own homes.

> In addition there is need for continual development, expansion, and application of knowledge and skill in working with disturbed parents and children to whom effective help cannot be given at present.

> Children should be separated from their parents only if family situations or problems of the children are such that with assistance, care and treatment cannot be obtained for the children while living at home.

> Even when family environments are unfavorable, or adversely affect children's development, children may still have strong ties to their families.

> Inherent in residential care are at least two problems that affect every child: separation from his or her family, and entrance into a way of life that is not customary in our society. Separation from the family is socially and psychologically disruptive, and children can

feel very different from other children who are reared by their parents.

0.22 Selection of appropriate form of substitute care

If a child must be cared for away from the family, the particular needs and problems of both, which may change from time to time, should be the basis for deciding what kind of care is most suitable.

For the child whose needs can best be met through substitute family life and who can participate in family and community life, foster family care offers opportunities that are in accord with our family-centered society.

The agency-owned or agency-operated group home provides group care and treatment for certain children—particularly adolescents—and is useful as a transition between residential care and return to family life. It may be used in lieu of a child welfare residence for many children whose appreciation of reality is relatively intact and whose problems of impulse control are manageable.

Residential care has unique values for children with social, psychological, developmental, or physical problems that can be treated most effectively through group living and the comprehensive resources and services that residential care can make available.

Adoption should be considered as early as possible for children whose parents will, in all probability, be unable to give them the care, support, and protection they need; or are unable or unwilling to accept parental responsibilities or to use the help of community resources in order to do so; or when the whereabouts of parents are unknown and they have maintained no responsible, continuing contact with their child.

Child Development

Advances in knowledge about children's growth and development and about the effect on human personality and behavior of multiple interrelated biological, social, cultural, and other environmental forces have brought about changes in the care of children.

0.23 Care based on needs of children

Certain principles have evolved from enhanced understanding of the needs of all children for love, care, protection, and esteem; for play, learning, social and spiritual experiences appropriate to their level of development; for training, guidance, and control; and for relationships with adults they can trust and with whom they can identify as models.

Affection and loving care should be essential elements of daily living, in an environment that conveys a feeling of personal concern for each child.

Receiving recognition encourages feelings of self-worth and adequacy. The child can become aware of individual differences, as well as interdependence, with others. Respect helps a child feel like an important member of the group in his or her own right and own way.

The way in which children are grouped and staff members selected offers opportunities for the children to learn to form relationships with a variety of persons.

Residential care must provide rich and stimulating living experiences that promote growth and development.

Because security, continuity, and stability are essential, each child must have continuing, consistent relationships with adults over a period of time. No child should be subjected to frequent staff turnover and to repeated change of placement. When change is desirable, preparation should help the child to be ready for it.

1

THE RESIDENTIAL CENTER AS A CHILD WELFARE SERVICE

The residential center is a child welfare service that provides 24-hour care for a child in a residential facility designed as a therapeutic environment. Within this setting are integrated treatment services, educational services, and group living on the basis of an individual plan for each child who cannot be effectively helped in his or her own home, with a substitute family, or in a less intensive group setting.

Goal of Residential Centers

The goal of residential centers is for every child to return to life in the community with improved ability to cope and succeed, either with his or her own family or a substitute family, in a group home or, for the older youth, independent living. Residential services should be planned with a foreseeable termination. Prolonged or indefinite periods of residential care are not acceptable practice.

1.1 Purpose

The purpose of residential service should be to provide group care and treatment for children whose needs cannot at the time be adequately met in a family; and to offer opportunities for a variety of experiences, through a group living program and treatment services, that can be selectively used in accordance with an individualized plan for each child to foster normal maturation. This is achieved by:

- correcting or modifying the effect of unsatisfactory experiences
- ameliorating social, behavioral, and emotional problems that interfere with the child's development and functioning

1.2 Responsibility of residential centers

The residential center should provide a concentrated, time-limited, therapeutic environment that includes group living for children and treatment services for them and their families.

The children placed in the center may have limited ability to contend with more complex surroundings. They require planned, carefully organized, and predictable surroundings with care and treatment that promote growth and development so that they can return to their communities.

Centers differ in the design of their programs and services. Each center must continually reexamine the treatment approaches it offers and the kind of environment it provides, if it is to achieve its objective in meeting the needs of the children served. (9.78)

1.3 Children for whom residential care is appropriate

Residential care should be used for children over 6 years of age whose relationships with adults and peers, level of development, and social and emotional problems require intensive and specialized services in a specially structured group environment.

These children fall into the following groups (which are not mutually exclusive):

- who have major difficulties in relating to adults or other children
- who have experienced much deprivation, rejection, neglect, or abuse in their own families or repeated separation experiences or unsatisfactory re-placements
- whose experiences have damaged their capacity to relate constructively to others
- who are withdrawn and have difficulty in responding to others
- who are fearful of forming relationships and are distrustful of any dependent relationship with an adult
- who are distrustful of authority and regard adult control as rejection

- whose behavior cannot be tolerated or modified in a family community
- who have not learned to control their impulses as expected at their age level
- who act out their problems in ways that are dangerous to themselves or others and who require special protection and control

1.4 Service as related to characteristics of children

Characteristics of children for whom residential care is to be provided, such as age, ethnicity, special needs, as well as particular social and emotional problems and family situations, should be the basis for determining type of program, staffing, special services, and facilities required. (1.2)

Services limited to a particular age group, such as adolescents, or children with particular problems, such as behavior disorders and disabling handicaps, often require adaptations and special provisions.

Services for children who are not part of the prevailing culture or race, or who speak a different language, will also require program and staff emphasis to make sure that children and families do not experience a sense of alienation or a limited use of agency service.

Programming must provide for a range of problems commonly found among young children referred for residential care: disturbances in feelings about themselves and others due to separation from significant persons or to repeated re-placements; interpersonal and intrapersonal difficulties developed over a period of time, resulting from deprivation and previous unmet needs, or reactive to the situation, e.g., parental difficulties culminating in the need for placement. These may be manifested in symptoms such as:

- difficulty in conforming to authority
- problems in relation to authority
- feelings of anxiety, guilt, hostility; lack of trust, lack of a sense of personal identity
- behavior disorders: lying, stealing, violent temper outbursts, fire setting, destructiveness, aggressive behavior
- learning disturbances, reading disabilities, low educational achievement
- inadequate development of self-control and skills, speech disturbances, nightmares, soiling and enuresis

Disturbances in parental functioning and other stress situations in the family that affect the child include:

- absence or impaired functioning of parents due to death; mental or physical illness; personality disorders; handicap; divorce; desertion
- inability of parents to cope with the particular problems of the child
- chronic disturbance or disruption of family life and lack of care and protection for the vulnerable child
- deprivation of opportunities for learning and constructive emotional experiences due to family problems, insufficient or unstable income, minority status, inadequate housing

1.5 Core components in residential services

Regardless of the type of residential center, care of children should have certain core components that can be used differentially according to the needs and problems of individual children and their families:

A procedure for assessment of the appropriateness of the care (1.7, 2.1–2.11);

A process of separation from his or her own home and of placement in a group of unrelated children (2.12, 2.17);

A group setting characterized by:

- peer groups and their influence
- a range of adults related to the children in a professional or staff capacity, with training and/or personal qualities qualifying them to deal with children (9.42–9.65)
- a physical facility owned and operated by an established organization (8.1–8.38)

A group living program purposely planned to provide:

- day-by-day living experiences conducive to growth and corrective of previous unsatisfactory experiences (3.14–3.28)
- individualization (1.8)
- an atmosphere favorable to children and their parents (0.6)
- tolerance and understanding of the feelings and behavior of unhappy or disturbed children (0.10)

Provisions for meeting normal dependency and developmental needs and specialized treatment needs common to children in residential care:

- child care (3.14–3.28)
- health service (2.19, 3.29–3.43)

18

- specialized medical services, when needed (3.41–3.43)
- recreation (3.47–3.50)
- religion (3.51–3.53)
- community participation (3.54)
- social work service (6.2–6.15, 3.46)
- education (4.3–4.12)
- psychological services (3.45)
- psychiatric services (3.44)
- life skills (5.2–5.8)

An individual treatment plan formulated for each child and his or her family as the basis for a coordinated approach by all staff working with them, including specific expectations that are consonant with the goal of service for the child and a plan for the child upon discharge. (2.13–2.16)

Treatment planning and review including the opinions of the child, participation of the family, involved staff members, and a representative of the agency that carries responsibility to act on behalf of the child. (2.2, 2.15)

1.6 Total service

The total service should have the following definable units of service:

Intake
- admissions study by the referral agency (2.1)
- placement study (2.7–2.9)
- decision to use the service (2.10)
- preparation for placement (2.12)

Services for children in care
- establishment of an individual treatment plan (2.13)
- implementation of the treatment plan for the child and systematic adjustment as needed (2.14, 2.15)
- services for the parents (2.16)

Termination
- discharge planning (2.24, 2.25)
- followup service upon discharge from 24-hour care (2.26)

1.7 Treatment plan

Treatment should provide for each child such help as he or she may need with his or her particular problems, on the basis of a purposeful plan arrived at by conscious deliberation of the staff team and with responsibility delegated to an appropriate staff member for integrating the total service for and with the child. (2.9)

> Treatment implies an intent to bring about some change in the problems of the child and in his or her family situation. It must be designed in accordance with the agency's philosophy of treatment and a diagnostic evaluation of the particular needs of the individual child and his or her family. (0.15)

> Use should be made of component parts of the service selectively, in accordance with the plan, so that they may reinforce each other at a given time.

> All parts of the program and services affecting the total life of the child should be coordinated.

> The approach of all staff members working with a particular child and his or her family should be harmonious, with a common goal and understanding of their respective responsibilities and roles in relation to the child and one another.

> Administration should assure implementation of the treatment plan.

1.8 Integration of services

The daily activities, group living program, educational program, and services designated in the plan for the individual child and the family should be coordinated and integrated into a unified approach to the child and parents that will have an impact on the problems and stimulate improvement in family functioning. (9.18)

> Integration can be achieved through regularly scheduled case conferences attended by all staff members who work with a particular child and family. (9.19)

> The family as well as the legal custodian (if one has been appointed) should be included in these conferences.

> Planning for each child and periodic progress evaluation should be based on contributions of all staff members working with the child and parents. (2.14, 2.15)

> When two or more agencies share responsibility for service to the child and family, representatives of both agencies have to be in constant communication to ensure an integration of services. (2.2)

1.9 Team approach

A team approach should be used in providing services in behalf of individual children.

Residential services require the contributions of various categories of staff with different training, backgrounds, and skills.

Each staff member must have a clearly defined role and responsibility, related to specific training and competence. (9.34)

Each staff member must be ready to carry out a designated role for the total service and must be able to understand the perspectives of other staff members and respect their particular competence and contributions. (2.14)

All staff members working with a child and family must be prepared to accept a common goal, use consultation, and be guided by an understanding of the needs, strengths, and problems of the child.

An atmosphere of mutual respect and trust throughout the staff is essential.

Unless specifically contraindicated, the parents should take part in and work closely with members of the treatment team in planning, evaluation conferences, and decision making. (2.6, 2.14, 2.15)

1.10 Protection of the rights of the child

When the agency makes a professional judgment that residential services are the most appropriate services for a child, the agency has a responsibility to recognize and maintain the rights of the child.

Acceptance of a child into residential care places the agency in a controlling position and should be made only after thorough consideration of other alternatives at a particular time. (2.1, 2.10)

It is essential to ensure the rights of a child to:
- services that preclude any form of discrimination on the basis of race or nationality (1.5, 10.3, 10.4)
- adequate nutrition, clothing, housing, recreation, medical services (3.14–3.28, 3.30, 3.47–3.49)
- care and guidance by adults who provide support and supervision in a reasonable and appropriate manner (5.2–5.8)
- protection from neglect, cruelty, and exploitation (3.1)
- education, training, and career guidance (3.24–3.26, 4.3, 4.7, 4.9)
- safe and clean surroundings that include provisions for personal privacy (3.13, 8.6–8.14)
- consideration of a child's personal opinions in decisions that affect his or her life (2.13, 2.14, 9.20)
- religious observance of choice (2.21, 3.51)
- respect for and understanding of the child's own ethnic and religious characteristics (1.5)

2

TOTAL SERVICES FOR CHILD AND PARENTS

The agency offering residential services should be responsible for administration of its total service. It is responsible for ensuring that gaps in service for the child and family do not occur. It should be connected with other services for children established within the agency or by formal agreement with other agencies.

2.1 Referral for service

The program of a residential center should begin with a referral that makes clear that other possibilities for care of the child have been considered, and that also includes a plan for stable care of the child after discharge from the center and completion of its service to the child and family.

Ordinarily the child is referred by another service of the agency, or an agency in the community that can call on the broad spectrum of services available. The referral should provide full information about the child and family, and the problems and circumstances that prompted the referral. (2.7)

A residential center should be used only when it is the most appropriate form of care and treatment for a particular child. Discussion with the parents before placement should focus on whether the home can be maintained for the child. If the latter question cannot be answered before placement, it should be answered as soon as possible after placement. (2.9)

It should be determined from the referral that other resources and services have been considered and explored. The residential center has the responsibility for deciding which children it should accept and under what conditions.

2.2 Responsibility of public agency that requests placement of a child

The public agency that acts on behalf of a child should, when requesting placement, plan with the other agency and agree mutually about the need for residential care and for coordination of joint responsibilities.

The joint responsibilities should be set forth in detail, e.g., the participation of the placing agency's representative in case conferences, the extent of the placing agency's continuing responsibility for the child, etc. (2.13–2.15)

On occasion, the public agency makes a contractual agreement with the parents that spells out the rights and responsibilities of the parents and the public agency. In such instances, the residential center should be fully informed. (2.23)

In some instances, the placement of a child is part of a more complex plan for service for a family that is already receiving services from another agency. It is essential to develop a means of coordination so that the family, as a whole, has an integrated service plan.

If the needs of the child are so specialized that an interstate placement is sought, there must be compliance with all requirements of the Interstate Compact on the Placement of Children. It is also necessary to ensure the quality of services for the child and family, as described in state licensing standards or regulations.

2.3 Referrals from court

If a child is committed to the agency by court, the referral should serve as the basis for the agency and the court to arrive at a mutual understanding of the child's needs and circumstances and of the plan for care and treatment of the child.

2.4 Emergency placement

Emergency placement in residential centers should be avoided; when, under extreme circumstances, an intake study cannot be made before placement, it should be carried out as soon as possible after admission.

It is essential that a child not remain in placement simply because of an initial emergency. The child should have immediate evaluation and planning to meet the problem.

Each community should have a range of resources, including 24-hour care, that are immediately available for children who lack care or are in danger, or when unexpected circumstances occur.

Because of the lack of emergency care facilities in some communities, residential centers have served as emergency shelters for dependent and delinquent children. This can be a bona fide function of residential centers only if emergency care is sufficiently separated from the regular program so that they do not hinder each other's progress or confuse the children about the purpose of their stay.

2.5 Purpose of intake study

There should be a defined procedure for study and evaluation of the needs and problems of the child and the parents to:

- help parents clarify the problem, what help is needed, and what they expect the service to accomplish for them and for the child
- assess the needs of the child and family
- assess the potential of the family for carrying out their child care responsibilities and for using available help to do so
- obtain information for a tentative plan for the child
- determine whether separation of the child from the family is necessary
- develop an estimate of the probable outcome of placement and its duration, with the participation of the parents and child, as well as the referring agency that is acting on behalf of the child. (2.9)

If it is desirable for a child to remain at home with the family, all necessary social services should be available to carry out such a plan. (2.10, 6.4)

If a child needs and is ready for a familial placement but the parents persist in requesting residential care, they should be helped to accept an appropriate plan for the child.

Help should be given to the parents and child as they consider their problems and the possible means by which these may be resolved, regardless of whether services of the agency will subsequently be used.

2.6 Participation of child and family in intake and treatment planning

The parents and the child should be helped to participate in decisions about the appropriateness of plans for placement and treatment.

Participation will vary from one child to the next, depending on age, maturity, etc.

The nature of family relationships and the circumstances necessitating placement will affect the extent of participation of the child or family.

In situations where parents are unavailable or unable to assume responsibility for decisions, or when the parent-child relationship is too disturbed or is dissolved, the legal guardian or placing agency has a special responsibility to safeguard the interests of the child.

2.7 Nature of intake study

The intake study should be a dynamic process, coordinated by the social worker.

Even if the child and parents have no part in the decision about what will happen, clear, supportive interpretation should be offered. In addition, their feelings and knowledge about the situation should be explored. (2.5, 2.12–2.14)

The parents and the child should be given information about the agency's services, policies, and procedures, including their legal rights and responsibilities and all that is involved for them if the child is accepted for placement and during the course of the service.

The intake worker should obtain the information pertinent to understanding the problem and reaching a joint decision with the parents and the referring agency regarding the appropriate service.

2.8 Pertinent information about child and family

The following information about the child is necessary:

Characteristics of the child: age, ethnicity, current developmental level (physical, social, intellectual, and emotional) and deviations from what is considered normal at that age; functioning at home, with peers, and in other significant life situations; ability to cope with his or her circumstances; ability to cope with life tasks expected of children of that age; nature of the child's relationship to the parents and other family members; capacity to form close relationships with adults and peers; degree of health and pathology in the personality structure; understanding of current situation and reaction to it.

Social work, psychological, or psychiatric services the child has received for help with his or her emotional problems.

Developmental history from birth to present: health history, **rate of progress**, developmental problems; past experiences that **may have** affected the child's development; previous placements by **the** parents or others (with dates), information about the child's adjustment, and reason for termination of each placement.

Current medical status including the use of drugs. (3.31, 3.32)

Legal status: names and addresses of person, persons, or agency having legal custody and guardianship, and the extent, if any, of court jurisdiction.

Education: grade level functioning, intellectual potential, grade level placement, existence of learning difficulties, previous educational functioning. (4.4)

The following information about the parents is necessary:

Family circumstances: constellation of family group; current situation (social, financial, emotional, health factors) as it affects the parents' ability to care for the child; problems that may have affected the child's development and may influence the outcome of the plan for placement (e.g., return to family, extended foster care, termination of parental rights); relationship of each parent to the child, to one another, and to other children in the family; potential of the parents or other significant family members for meeting the child's needs and their accessibility for help.

Parents' expectations of placement: help requested for the child and themselves; other solutions attempted; degree to which the parents can be involved, the role they see for themselves and significant family members while the child is receiving care; their plan for, and understanding of, length of stay and termination; the way in which they are preparing the child for placement. (2.13, 2.14, 6.2, 6.3)

2.9 Sources of information

The parents and the child should be the primary sources of information; pertinent information available from other sources should be requested, with respect for confidentiality.

In addition to the referral data, other sources include:

- significant family members outside the immediate family, and foster parents
- teachers and other school personnel
- other social agencies, psychiatric or mental health facilities, courts, health agencies
- reports from physicians, including psychiatrists, and psychologists

Parents should be told when information is being shared or requested and should be asked for their written consent.

Psychological testing and psychiatric examination should be arranged when needed to arrive at an understanding of the nature and severity of the child's personality problems. (3.44, 3.45)

2.10 Decision to accept the child

The decision to accept the child for residential care and the plan for treatment should be arrived at jointly by the staff carrying responsibility for the various divisions of the service, with the executive, or designee, carrying responsibility for the final decision. (3.31, 3.44, 4.2, 5.1, 7.2, 9.15, 9.39, 9.40)

It is important for the staff members who will be involved with the child to participate in the process of making this decision. The decision must include an evaluation of the following essentials:

- the inability of the parents to give the child the care needed
- the likelihood that the child will benefit by placement and be helped with his or her problems through group care
- the likelihood that the child will profit from the services the agency has available and from the particular group in which the child can be placed
- the capacity of the parents to use help to carry, resume, or relinquish their responsibilities
- the probable outcome as to return to the child's family, another placement, adoption, or for the adolescent, a group home or independent living

The decision must be concurred in by the parents (unless limited by the court), the agency that is to provide the care, and the agency that carries a legal responsibility for the child.

2.11 Referral to another agency

If the child or the family requires a service other than a residential center and the agency does not offer it, recommendations should be made to the referral source or referral made to the appropriate resource. (7.4)

If another agency will provide services to the family while the child is in care, frequent communication between the agencies should begin at intake and continue on a planned and regular basis. Any proposed changes in the plan should be discussed as soon as possible.

Preparation for Placement

2.12 Preparation of child for placement

The child should be prepared for placement and admission to the residential center through planned procedures, giving him or her the opportunity to understand what is happening and to be able to cope with the new situation. (6.1, 6.3, 7.5, 7.6)

The child should have help from the parents, or parental surrogate, and from the social worker who will work with the child and the family after admission. The more that parents can be helped to take responsibility for preparation, the easier it will be for the child to accept placement.

Preparation for placement will vary with each child and should be adapted to the age, experience, individual needs, and personality of the child; to the circumstances necessitating placement; and to special problems presented by the prospect of placement.

Arrangements should be made for a medical examination. (3.34)

Timing of placement should be adapted to the child's tempo of assimilating new and disturbing experiences and should allow the child sufficient time to master the various steps of the placement process. This fulfills one of the basic requirements for learning and growth, since the child is strengthened by successful mastery of tasks and is weakened each time he or she is overwhelmed by and unable to cope successfully with a new experience.

Every effort should be made to have the child meet his or her social worker during intake.

Whenever possible, arrangements should be made for the child to visit the residential center one or more times before admission, in order to become familiar with the new situation and to have opportunities to met the child care workers and other staff members who may be important to the child in the group living experience. If parents can be supportive, it is desirable for them to accompany the child during the visit.

Administration and child care staff should plan for reception of the child. Staff members who will be involved in working with the child should be told the time and date of arrival so that they may meet the child and parents, have the room prepared, and have a place ready in the living group and in school. (4.3, 5.3, 6.5)

The other children in the group to which the child is assigned should be prepared for the child's arrival.

Services for the Child in Placement

2.13 Setting service goals and objectives

The referral source and the staff team should reach an understanding with the child and the parents about specific goals for the use of the services of the center, after taking into consideration the nature of the problem, the capacities of the child and parents, and their motivation to deal with specific conditions, circumstances, and their social situation.

Mutual objectives, in writing, established for the child and family, should be related to the improvement in social functioning of the child and the family and promotion of the child's development.

For the child and family, such goals and objectives can make possible a common understanding with the agency about what does or should occur, the ways in which expectations will be met, and thus a sense over time of whether progress is being made to effect a desired result.

Descriptive measures and criteria for measuring attainment of the goals have the advantage of clear expectations that are understood by the child, the family, and the staff.

2.14 Making a service plan

Components of a service plan should include:
- short-term and long-term objectives and priorities during care, includ-ing prolonged length of stay and the service eventuality
- a written contract (or agreement), established between the parents, the child, and the center that describes the therapeutic approach and expectations (2.22)

- decisions about the group in which the child lives (3.3)
- relationships with specific staff members to be encouraged and developed
- a defined though flexible relationship between the child and parents (e.g., visits, telephone calls, home visits, written correspondence)
- recreational activities for the child
- educational program for the child (4.4)
- designation of staff responsibility for work with parents and for direct treatment of the child (1.10)

> All staff members who are or will be involved in working with the child and parents should take part in making the plan. (1.8, 1.9)
>
> When the referring agency carries legal responsibility for the child, its participation in this planning is essential. (2.2)

2.15 Quarterly evaluation

The progress of each child and family and the treatment plan should be evaluated at least quarterly in case conferences attended by all staff members who worked with the child and family, and other agency staff members when appropriate.

> Measures of progress toward short-term and long-term objectives should be fully discussed by all participants and new objectives established as needed to achieve designated goals.
>
> Changes in the treatment plan may differ from the original agreement of service for the child and family. The parents, staff, and child, when old enough, should sign the revised plan. (2.13, 2.23)
>
> A summary of each conference, including recommendations and revisions of the plan, should be included in the case record. The social worker should carry responsibility for maintaining the agency record, which is kept in one specified location in the residential center. (6.16)

Services for Parents

> Because of what the child and family mean to each other, the service, to be of benefit, must include the whole family. (6.11, 6.15)

2.16 Purpose of services for parents

Services for parents should be an essential part of residential care:

- to preserve the child-parent relationship to the fullest extent
- to enable parents to perform their parental role as fully as they can
- to give parents the opportunity to exercise their legal rights and responsibilities in ways compatible with the child's welfare, unless it becomes necessary in the interest of the child to seek abridgment of them
- to ensure the earliest appropriate implementation of a permanent plan for the child
- to ensure their participation in the child's treatment and to understand the interactionist nature of their relationship and their responsibility in the development of the child's problems

> The relationship between the child and his or her siblings, and the meaning and effect of the separation upon both, are also important in the treatment plan.

2.17 Participation of parents in the placement

Parents should be helped to use every opportunity to maintain their relationship with the child and to participate in making the placement possible and constructive for him or her. (2.6, 2.12–2.15, 6.1, 6.4, 6.10, 6.11–6.15)

> The parents' ability to continue their contacts and relationship with the child should be one of the factors considered in the decision to accept the child for care. In addition to social and emotional factors, the possibility of the parents traveling to visit the child (in relation to distance, health, financial means, and other responsibilities) and the child's ability to visit the parents should be taken into consideration in developing the plan for service.

> Even if at the time of placement it may seem a better solution for a child not to return to the family home, nevertheless, in considering the total effect on the child, it is usually better for the child when the parents are included in the service, participate within their ability, and remain a part of the child's life. (2.12–2.15)

> Parents should be informed of and helped to understand the conditions of placement, and to take such responsibility for participation during the placement of their child as they are able to carry. (2.23)

> Parents should also be encouraged to take part in holiday celebrations and other events in the life of the child, as well as arrange for periodic or regular visits of the child in their home, unless limited by judicial decision or by the plan of service for the child. (2.22)

Parents should be encouraged to participate in varying ways in the daily life of the child in the center. Staff training is focused on making therapeutic use of the parents' presence and activity.

2.18 Protection of parental rights

The parents should be protected in the exercise of their legal rights or responsibilities to the child, except when there is evidence of their inability to assume the parental role adequately and society must intervene to protect the child and promote his or her well-being. (9.21–24)

Whether parents voluntarily decide on placement for the child and agree to use agency services for this purpose, or whether their child is committed to the agency by the court, they have inherent rights and responsibilities that must be respected.

At the same time, they must be helped to recognize that the agency must assume certain parental functions while the child is receiving care and treatment in the residential center. (2.22)

When it becomes necessary to delegate or transfer any of the legal rights of parents to the agency having responsibility for the child, it is important to clarify, and to help parents understand, the legal rights and obligations that they retain, as well as those that the parents or court delegate to the agency. (9.22–9.23)

When parents enter into a voluntary agreement with a child welfare agency for placement of their child, they retain their full rights and duties, with the exception of those that they agree to delegate to the agency and that the agency undertakes to provide in their stead. In situations of voluntary placement, the parents have the full right to have the child returned to them upon request. If the agency decides that it is contrary to the welfare of the child to permit discharge, it has the responsibility to institute proper legal action. (9.21, 9.24)

Even after a court has vested legal custody or guardianship of the child's person in the agency, and unless the parent-child relationship has been terminated by judicial decree, the parent retains certain residual rights, which often include reasonable visitation, information about the child's whereabouts and condition, consent to adoption, inheritance, the right to notice of and appearance at judicial proceedings involving the child, and in many jurisdictions, determination of religious affiliation. Responsibility for support usually follows. (9.22)

If it is determined that the child's best interests can be served only when the parents' legal rights are limited or terminated through court action, the agency should discuss it in advance with the parents and take the initiative in presenting such a recommendation to the child's legal guardian or the appropriate court, with a statement of the facts upon which it is based. (2.15, 6.13, 8.24)

2.19 Responsibility for medical and dental care

Responsibility for medical and dental care should be delegated to the agency. Consent for routine medical and emergency surgical care and hospitalization should be given in writing by the parents, or if their rights are limited, the court. (2.22, 9.21)

Parents should be given assurance that only in the event of an emergency will major surgery or treatment be authorized for a child without prior consultation with them, so long as they are available.

2.20 Responsibility to support

Parents should be expected to contribute to the cost of the child's care according to their ability to do so. (9.11)

Financial contribution to the child's support can serve to maintain a bond between parents and child, and can be used as a tool in treatment for the parents. (6.11)

The amount to be paid should be determined on the basis of a budgetary guide or other criterion of ability to pay, taking into consideration family income and other resources, financial obligations, and needs of other members of the family.

2.21 Determination of religious affiliation

Parents (or in some jurisdictions, the court) have the right to designate the religious affiliation of the child, including the right to have no religious affiliation. (3.51)

The adolescent may have the right to choose his or her own religion.

2.22 Contact between children and parents

The parents have a right to reasonable visiting privileges unless curtailed by judicial action.

Regular contacts between parents and child should be encouraged, unless it is contraindicated by the treatment plan. Siblings should also be included in the visiting plan. The residential center should be near enough to the child's home for parents to visit. If travel costs are problematic for the family, the agency should explore possible resources (including the resources of the agency) to maintain a visiting plan.

Visiting hours should be flexible for parents who are unable to come at designated times.

Staff should observe the effects of contacts between the child and parents. One or the other or both may need help to face the realities of their circumstances and their feelings, and to handle the difficulties that may arise.

No child should be deprived of contacts with parents simply because the parents cannot or do not want to use help for themselves, because they do not pay for the child's care, or because the child is being punished.

Comfortable facilities should be available for parents to see their children at the center, with some privacy. If parental responsibilities are carried by older brothers or sisters, or by other relatives or foster parents, they should be encouraged to visit and to maintain a relationship with the child.

In the case of foster parents, their continuing role in terms of visiting and possible return of the child to the foster home should be clarified through collaboration between the agency they served and the agency caring for the child.

Children should visit with their family at home in accordance with the treatment plan.

2.23 Written agreement

When the child is accepted for care, a written contract between parents and agency should be prepared and signed by the parents and by the social worker, as the agency representative. The agreement should be filed in the case record and a copy given to the family. (2.14, 2.15)

This statement can be the responsibility of the public agency that carries a legal responsibility for the child. In such instances the agency that has the legal responsibility makes an agreement with the agency providing care for the child. (2.2)

The contract should cover the responsibility of the parents and the agency, and conditions under which service will be given, including at least:

• responsibility for financial support (2.20)
• arrangements for medical care (2.29)

- visiting regulations and expectations (2.22)
- arrangements for clothing allowances
- arrangements for vacations
- regulations about gifts permitted
- arrangements for parents' participation through regularly scheduled interviews with social workers and participation in case conferences (2.13–2.15)
- use of any physical discipline or restraint (3.25)
- the requirement in voluntary placements that the child may be removed from the center by the parents only after a prior agreement with the agency and with sufficient advance notice so that child and agency can be suitably prepared.

The agreement should make the parents aware that every effort will be made by the agency to have the child return home, but in the event that this objective proves unattainable, other plans for a stable living situation may be necessary, including appropriate legal action for permanent separation. (9.24)

Discharge and Aftercare Services

2.24 Discharge

The decision that the child no longer needs or can benefit by residential services and is ready to leave should be reached in a joint conference of the child and family with those staff members who are directly involved in the care and treatment of the child and family. The executive carries final responsibility in this decision-making process, but may designate an appropriate staff member to fulfill the agency's responsibility.

It is extremely important to keep in mind that adjustment to the residential center and the program should not be considered as the indicator of the child's capacity to adjust to the external community.

The duration of treatment and the ultimate outcome of the service should be determined by the nature of the child's assets and problems, the child's progress in use of the services, the family situation, strengths and limitations of the parents, the treatment plan, and the availability of suitable resources in the community.

2.25 Preparation for termination of residential service

The child and the family should have participated in planning the services and the discharge, whether to the own home or other arrangement. As the termination of the placement approaches, they should have additional help and support.

All staff members who are in direct contact with the child should assist in preparing him or her for leaving. While discharge from the residential center is the realization of a goal, the child, family, and staff generally have mixed feelings. The value of an integrated team approach is best realized in a gradual acceptance of the discharge.

Preparation should be a process allowing the child to test his or her experience and ease through gradually extended contacts with his or her own family, in a foster family or group home or other living arrangement.

Time will be needed for the child to make new friends and for the child and family to plan for changing relationships with the residential center, which may include return visits to the center and continued treatment.

The legal guardian or the agency that carries legal responsibility for the child should be involved in the discharge phase to assist in orderly planning for the child and family.

The educational placement of the child must be considered and clarified in the discharge plan.

If the plan is for a further placement rather than return home, there should be extensive joint preparation between the old and new agency.

If the child is to live with a foster family, in a group home, or in another residential facility, he or she should have the opportunity to visit with the foster parents or with new staff, and should have a preliminary visit to the new home or facility.

For the older child who will become independent, considerable support and practical assistance should be provided before and after departure from the center so that the young person can become established.

2.26 Aftercare

The residential center should assure the child and family that help will be provided until the discharge plan is fully carried out.

The child should be discharged from supervision when:
- with the family and making a satisfactory adjustment
- legally adopted and making a satisfactory adjustment

- capable of self-support
- another agency has accepted responsibility

If the court should request the agency to continue supervision of the child in his or her own home after the commitment for residential care is terminated, a determination of the child's and parents' willingness to use this service should be made and a definite time limit set with the court.

Aftercare service in return to the own home or in independent living should provide active help to the parents and the child during the period of adjustment. The staff has a responsibility to assist the child and family to obtain needed community resources, including recreation, appropriate educational placement, and other basic services.

3

PROGRAM FOR CARE

Children living together in groups have needs for growth and development that are common to all children, as well as the special needs and problems for which they require treatment and residential care.

The program of residential service should provide for:

- planning and coordination of the child's daily living experiences and activities with specialized services for treatment
- a variety of rich and stimulating experiences not available in other types of placement
- opportunities ordinarily available to children living in their own families: daily care, health care, education, religion, recreation, and family and community contacts

3.1 Basis for program

The program should be based on the needs of the kind of children for whom the agency undertakes to provide care and treatment, taking into account their age, sex, intelligence, family situation, problems, and other characteristics.

A child should not have to fit into a program that is not able to meet his or her particular needs.

Group Living Program

The group living program provides a structure within which the environment can be adapted and modified to meet the individual and group needs of children. It should be purposely planned so that each child has opportunities to use selectively a wide range of experiences. (0.4)

Many groups are formed spontaneously by the children themselves. Certain groups should be intentionally planned and constructed to give children certain kinds of experiences according to their particular needs. The essential ones are: the living group, the activity group, and the treatment group.

3.2 Grouping

The composition of each living group should be purposely planned and periodically evaluated. Each center should have certain principles as the basis for assigning children to the living group, but should at the same time allow for experimentation.

The most important planned group, not chosen by the child, is the living group: children who live together in the same physical unit and who eat, sleep, play, and work together under the supervision of two or more child care staff members.

Children should be placed in the group that will best meet their needs, taking into consideration such matters as interaction between and among children in the group, possible effect of the particular child on the group, and degree and kind of group forces generated by the nature and size of a group. (3.4, 3.6–3.9)

It is important to study values and limitations of different kinds of grouping to gain more precise knowledge about group dynamics.

3.3 Responsibility for grouping

The staff member with responsibility for supervision of group living units should be responsible for formation of living groups and assignment of individual children to them, in consultation with other staff members working with the children involved.

3.4 Size of living group

The size of a living group should be determined by the nature and severity of the children's problems, their age, and the number of child care staff members available at all times.

There should normally be not more than 6–8 children in a living group. It must be small enough to allow maximum opportunity for:

- appropriate individualization of the child by the adult in charge
- close observation as a basis for continued and flexible planning for the child
- the child to feel security and comfort through knowing that the adult is physically close and available day and night
- the child to resolve individual and social conflicts at his or her own pace
- meaningful interaction of each child with other members of the group
- giving the child a feeling that he or she is important and special, yet part of the group
- the child to develop responsibility in carrying out activities of daily living
- flexible handling of routines

3.5 Staff coverage

The number of child care workers responsible for children in the living group should be determined by the age and problems of the children. (8.32)

Working hours for child care staff should be scheduled according to the needs of the children, with allowances for time off, holidays, and vacations. Night as well as day coverage is essential so that the children can be assured of help and protection whenever they need it. The same team of child care workers should be assigned to a living group all the time.

There are certain high-sensitivity periods in the living group situation (e.g., after school, waking hours, meals, bedtime). During these periods of the day, more adults should be available in the living group, regardless of its size, to allow for individual attention. Recreation workers, volunteers, social workers, or teachers may augment the regular complement of child care staff.

When children are asleep, in school, or at activities, fewer staff members are needed, but one staff member should always be in the living group and on active duty at all times. When there are recurrent problems among the children in the living group, such as disruptive and destructive behavior, stealing, running away, sexual activity, wetting or soiling, more staff will be needed on a regular basis.

3.6 Grouping by age

Although there is no conclusive evidence to support grouping of children within a narrow or wide age range, it is generally considered preferable for the living group to be composed of children within a narrow age range.

It is recognized that there is a wide range of social, emotional, and intellectual maturity in any chronological age group. It is easier, however, to plan activities to meet the needs of the group when children are near enough in age to have similar interests and requirements.

As a rule, children prefer to be with others of about the same age.

Opportunity for relationships with children of differing ages, or of the same maturational level, can be given outside of the living group. (3.10)

3.7 Adolescent groups

A program for adolescents may be organized within a residential center by planning certain living units specifically for them.

Residential centers may design their programs specifically for adolescents.

Such programs should be planned with the differing needs and treatment goals of adolescents as the focus, i.e., experimenting with independence while having the security of being in a residential facility, opportunities for outside jobs and earning money, wider participation in the community, dating, etc.

3.8 Grouping by personality characteristics

It is generally not possible or desirable to group children on the basis of similar personality characteristics and problems.

3.9 Coeducational living groups

Placement of children and adolescents in coeducational living units should be decided on the basis of their emotional level and their problems, and their ability to adjust to a close living relationship with other boys and girls. Coeducational programs should be carefully planned in relation to the physical facilities of the living units, number and skills of staff members, and quality of supervision.

Group living for boys and girls together on the same campus or in the same unit has many advantages. It is one of the ways that our society prepares children for social interaction between men and women. The children can have a number of activities together, and experience healthy social interaction with each other.

When boys and girls live together, considerable tension may exist. This tension and the ensuing problems are usually related to underlying sexual tensions, which vary according to the ages, experiences, and nature of the emotional and social problems of the members of the group. Activities and group experiences must be planned carefully to promote development of healthy social relationships and to avoid undue demands on the ability of the children to withstand stimulation and contagion in this area.

Adolescents of the same sex are more suited to be together at this time than at any other time. They can grow best at their own pace in the society of their own sex.

Some adolescents may be too disturbed or emotionally labile to live in a coeducational facility.

3.10 Activity groups

Activity groups should be planned so that children have opportunities to interact with children of different ages and of both sexes, and to develop new interests and skills that help them gain self-confidence and acceptance by others.

The activity group may be larger than the living group and thus permit the child who is not ready for active participation to become part of a group at a slower, self-determined pace.

Activity groups may give children a choice of joining or not, whereas the children are assigned to the living group.

The child can have a variety of relationships with children and adults of both sexes, different ages, personalities, and skills, in addition to the more constant relation with the child care workers in his or her living group.

Initiation and termination can be timed according to the child's ability to tolerate one activity for a given period.

3.11 Group living as a treatment method

Use of groups for direct treatment of a child should be determined as a plan of service for each child. (1.7, 2.13–2.15, 3.2)

Some children who are not accessible to individual therapy at a particular time may be reached better through a group.

3.12 Size of residential center

It is desirable for a residential center to provide services for no more than 50 children; the total number of children in one group living program should not be so small that grouping is ineffective, nor so large that coordination, peer and staff interaction, and administrative supervision become difficult.

When the center has more than 50 children, it is difficult to prevent dilution of the skills, efforts, and collaboration of staff members in carrying out plans for individual children and their families.

The center with about 50 children is able to provide them with a broad range and variety of resources, activities, and services.

3.13 Safety

Adequate measures should be taken to remove safety hazards and to prevent accidents. (8.37–8.39)

Concern for safety should not cause agencies to unduly restrict or interfere with normal childhood activities.

Children with physical handicaps should be protected through appropriate and specific safety measures and equipment that allow them to participate appropriately in activities.

Active sports should be supervised by staff capable of handling emergencies; e.g., a lifeguard should be present when children are swimming; one or more staff members in the living unit should have training in first aid.

All children should be periodically instructed in fire prevention. Except for children who can carry responsibility, they should not be allowed to handle inflammable or combustible materials, use matches, or tend fires, unless they have close supervision.

The children and the staff should be given instructions about what to do in case of a fire or other emergencies, and should have drills at regular intervals. A comprehensive plan for fires and other disasters should outline what actions are to be taken by staff for the safety of the children and themselves. (8.39)

Poisons and medicines should be in a secure location. Prescribed medicines that will not be administered immediately (i.e., within the week), need not be stored in the living unit.

Daily Living Experiences

The program should provide conditions favorable to the individual development of children living in groups. While group care is not intended to reproduce family life, it should be possible for children to have many of the experiences and the things that families ordinarily provide to meet children's physical, emotional, and social needs, and to help them meet the expectations of social living. Such experiences should be corrective of previous unsatisfactory experiences.

3.14 Personal care

The individual needs of each child should be met on a daily basis with sufficient attention so that no child feels lost in the group.

Each child should have the personal help that all children need at times, regardless of age, in waking, dressing, deciding what to wear, combing hair, care of clothing, grooming, getting ready for meals or school, keeping appointments, going to bed.

Special attention and comforting are needed when a child is sick or upset.

Each child should be helped to assume responsibility for self-care.

Every child needs a caring adult with whom a relationship can develop that lets the child feel the adult's concern about his or her well-being. (5.3)

3.15 Controls*

The controls needed by children at any given time, which vary according to their age, maturational level, nature of behavior disturbances, and their particular group, should be provided by:
• plan and arrangement of physical facilities

---

* *Coping with Disruptive Behavior in Group Care*, by Eva M. Russo and Ann W. Shyne. Child Welfare League of America, 1980.

- organization of daily living program
- clear delegation to staff of defined adult responsibilities
- delimitation of those areas in which the children are able and free to make their own decisions

> Children need reasonable controls as an essential element for their development and treatment.

> For children to acquire and maintain appropriate inner controls, the environment must provide an orderly living situation and protective, supportive guidance from adults who respect them and whom they can respect and trust.

> Children should not be expected to assume controls in aspects of living for which they are not prepared, or for which society does not consider them ready.

> The adults in their lives must assume full responsibility for the limits that children have not as yet become capable of exercising. The plan for each child should include some assessment of his or her:

> - readiness and capacity to exercise self-control
> - degree of readiness to learn controls
> - need to rely on the adult for help in self-control
> - areas to which controls apply

> Different approaches are required for different kinds of children and groups. Specific rules and regulations should necessarily vary for different living groups and be adaptable to the group situations and the capacity and readiness of individual children to exercise self-control in specific areas.

3.16 Daily routines

The daily program should be planned to provide a consistent, well-structured, yet flexible framework for daily living, and should be periodically reviewed and revised as the needs of individual children or of the living group change. (1.9)

> Routines should be determined in relation to needs and convenience of both children and adults living together. The daily program should be comfortably relaxed yet stimulating and flexible, albeit balanced with sufficient routines and controls to give the child a sense of orderly living.

> Routines should be sufficiently adaptable to a particular child's physical and emotional capacity to conform to them, or to allow for special situations.

Variations in routines are desirable to prevent monotony. Rules and regulations should be kept to the minimum essential for the care and protection of the children and for consideration of others with whom they live, so that children can learn and understand the necessity and reasons for them.

Whenever appropriate, children and staff should have the opportunity of participating in deciding about routines and regulations, so that these may be more acceptable and effective.

3.17 Food

Planning, preparation, and serving of food should be in accordance with nutritional, social, and emotional needs of children in care.

Food has not only nutritional, but also social, educational, and therapeutic values. It is especially significant for children who have been malnourished or deprived of affection. The feeling that food tastes good contributes to the child's sense of well-being. The approach and methods used in providing food are extremely important in the care and treatment of each child, and can also be used to help a child develop orderly living habits. Mealtime should be a pleasurable experience in a relaxed atmosphere. The food should be well prepared, palatable, and attractively served. Dishes, flatware, napkins, and place mats or table cloths that add beauty and dignity to mealtime should be used.

Children should be encouraged rather than coerced to eat many different foods, with recognition of individual tastes and differences in quantity of food required.

The diet should include a variety of foods, menus, and snacks that provide the total daily nutritional requirements, and should be planned and prepared under the supervision of, or in consultation with, a dietitian or nutritionist who can arrange the special diets that some children require, and include some of the food preferences of the children of different cultural groups. (3.7, 8.13–8.14, 8.23, 9.43)

Sufficient quantity of food to allow for second helpings, snacks, celebrations, and outings should be provided. Snacks can be offered routinely after school and at bedtime. They represent adult concern and desire to care for and comfort the child.

The same food should be served to everyone, with the exceptions normally found in family life, such as when adults drink tea or coffee and when special diets are required.

It is preferable to have one person in charge of food service, who is familiar with nutrition, food service, and management. Food service records should be kept to assure compliance with nutritional needs of children and for administrative purposes.

3.18 Sleep

Routines in respect to getting up in the morning and going to bed should allow the children to have the amount of sleep and rest they require, and should be adapted to the age, physical condition, particular characteristics, problems, and school and work schedules of children in each group.

It is best to wake each child individually.

Evening activities should be planned that are not so stimulating as to keep children awake after the activity, and should take into consideration that children are in greatest need of reassurances at the end of the day.

Snacks before bedtime should be offered. (3.17)

Children who feel lonely and homesick, or who have sleep disturbances, need to have someone they know near them during the night. (3.5)

Children who need extra sleep, whose sleep is easily disturbed, or who need greater privacy because of their age, emotional upset, or adjustment problems should have single bedrooms. (8.7)

3.19 Grooming and personal hygiene

Standards of personal hygiene and grooming in relation to bathing, brushing teeth, care of hair and nails, toilet habits, should be maintained so that children can develop habits of personal care of their bodies, good grooming, and cleanliness as an accepted routine and a pleasurable experience.

3.20 Clothing

The agency should furnish each child with clothing selected and purchased especially for or by the child, similar in appearance, quality, and quantity to that worn by other children in the community.

Clothing contributes to the child's feeling of worth and dignity. It represents being valued by adults, respect for individuality, and having someone who cares for him or her. Clothing should be provided in a manner that helps the child develop self-esteem and a sense of personal responsibility.

Each child should have training and experience, according to age, in the selection and proper care of clothing. Children who are able to take part in budgeting for their clothes should be encouraged to do so. Adolescents should have clothing allowances and go shopping for their clothing alone or with peers, if they are capable, or with their child care worker or other adult.

Clothing should be becoming, of proper size, of the character usually worn by children in the area, and adequate in amount to permit laundering, cleaning, and repair. Shoes should be fitted to the individual child.

Each child should have closet and drawer space in the bedroom, and free access to his or her seasonal supply of clothing. (8.9)

3.21 Personal possessions

Each child should be allowed to bring personal possessions to the residential center and to acquire personal belongings.

The security of having and keeping possessions of one's own contributes to a sense of autonomy and identity. Children should have a safe place for their belongings. Individual storage space should be provided for their collections, play equipment, and other "treasures." Children with particularly valuable keepsakes may need staff help to keep them safe.

Each child should be able to feel, insofar as possible, that the bedroom is one's "own room." It should afford some degree of privacy and a place to keep personal possessions. The child should have an opportunity to participate in its decoration and in arranging the furniture and his or her own possessions. (8.9)

3.22 Allowances and money

Each child should be given a regular allowance in order to have the experience of possessing money and learning how to spend it appropriately.

Allowances should be on a scale according to age, similar to those that other children in the community receive. Older children should be given opportunities to earn additional money for their own use. (3.24)

It should be made clear to the child that he or she is responsible for meeting specific expenses that are agreed upon by the child and staff, e.g., incidental school expenses. An allowance should not include expenses the center should assume (e.g., unusual school expenditures, graduation expenses, confirmation clothes, scout or band uniforms).

Allowances should not be withheld or withdrawn as a means of punishment. Reasonable deductions, however, based on the amount of the allowance and the extent of damage, may be made to pay for damage done by the child.

3.23 Work assignments

Each child should be assigned daily or weekly chores that provide opportunities to learn to assume responsibility and to get satisfaction from contributing to work that must be done, according to age, health, interest, ability, and readiness.

Children should participate in selecting assignments and have a chance to work together and become familiar with a variety of tasks. They should understand why work must be done and be able to get a sense of satisfaction for themselves and recognition for their contribution.

The chores should be similar to those of children of families in the neighboring community.

Children should not be depended upon to do work for which staff should be employed.

There should be a limit on the amount of work expected: on an average, not more than 20 minutes a day for children under 12, and an hour for children over 12.

3.24 Payment for work

Children may be given jobs for which they receive payment, which should be clearly differentiated from duties expected of any child in the course of daily living.

Children should have help in learning how to budget, spend, and save the money that they earn.

The money children earn should be for their personal use.

Older children should be allowed to accept suitable employment in the community. Work experiences can offer opportunities to explore different kinds of work, to try occupational roles, and to begin to explore the values and behaviors expected of a worker in the community. Work should be done in compliance with the child labor laws and paid for according to community rates, to avoid exploitation.

Adolescents who want and can benefit from vocational training should have help in finding appropriate job opportunities that lead to vocational preparation. It is unwise, however, to let boys and girls in early adolescence make vocational choices that will limit their experience or education.

3.25 Discipline

Children should be given opportunities to learn gradually to assume responsibilities and make decisions for phases of daily living that they are able to carry out by themselves; they should have the assistance and guidance of adults whom they trust and respect, with whom they have a positive relationship, while learning self-control and self-direction in a widening sphere of daily life.

Discipline is the educational process by which adults help a child to have the experiences that enable the child to learn to live in reasonable conformity with accepted standards of social behavior, and to do so by progressively acquiring and applying self-control, rather than relying on external pressures. (3.15)

Every center should develop policies and procedures to govern all disciplinary actions. Staff should be fully aware of these policies and their implications through staff development and written materials.

Each child should know the basic rules that include not hurting others, not destroying things, not disrupting ongoing activities. Good discipline involves being clear and specific as to limits on behavior, showing the child what is permitted and what is not, and giving feedback on actions that are right or wrong.

Children develop inner controls by wanting to be like those they love and who love them, and to win their praise. They need the experience of being cared for by adults who give them a feeling of being understood, who offer continuing interest or support, and who have standards and values that children can try out and eventually incorporate themselves. Responsibility for discipline should be given to the child care worker who takes care of the children and supervises their daily activities. (5.6)

3.26 Misbehavior

To be effective, adult intervention should be determined by an understanding of the particular child, the immediate situation, the particular living group of the child, the child's capacity at the time to learn from the experience, and the treatment plan.

The adult must help each child develop patterns of behavior that foster constructive relationships and an increasing ability to deal with the expectations and requirements of daily life.

Misbehavior should be appraised and dealt with in a manner that promotes development of the child's inner controls and a sense of responsibility for his or her actions.

Each type of misbehavior requires a different approach and opportunity for the child to learn the different levels of control, depending on whether it involves:

- ineffective learning of controls in process of being acquired
- failure to live up to the child's capacity to exercise appropriate controls already acquired
- failure to recognize or accept authority carried by the adults in certain areas

Appropriate intervention may be:

- viewing the incident as an indication of the child's need for greater support and guidance, rather than as an occasion for censuring lack of self-control
- guidance to the child in living up to his or her capacities, allowing the opportunity to make mistakes without reproach, to have the incident overlooked, or to experience the consequences of his or her behavior as an essential learning experience
- dealing with situations in which children transgress the sphere of authority of adults primarily as an attempt to assume responsibilities prematurely, rather than as failure in carrying them out; such occurrences become a challenge to the adults to carry their responsibilities more effectively so that children will not need to try to take them over before they are capable

Some situations require purposeful noninterference, i.e., nothing should be done. Others call for active intervention, such as reasoning and discussion of the incident, changing the situation, disapproval, physical restraint, or punishment.

Sometimes removal from the group and group activities is necessary for a time, to protect the child from hurting himself or herself or others, or to limit disruption of the group. When removal is determined to be the most advisable form of interference, it should be handled as isolation from a situation. An adult must be with the child to make sure the child does not seriously hurt himself or herself and to let the child know and experience the adult's continuing wish to help.

Talking with an adult about misbehavior, and explaining what happened, its causes and consequences, and how one might have chosen a more appropriate course of action, can help a child understand the situation, achieve self-control, and internalize standards. Constructive discipline protects the child's security and self-esteem.

Repeated incidents requiring disciplinary action may be prevented by systematic evaluation to determine whether the atmosphere of the center, attitudes and expectations of the adults and their relationship to the children, and the center's grouping and programming may contribute to their occurrence.

3.27 Punishment

Punishment should be used only in situations where other means are ineffective and when children can benefit by the experience of facing the consequences of unacceptable behavior, not as an end in itself, but as part of a learning process.

Punishment is one form of intervention by the adult in situations in which the child fails to behave as expected or required, or to maintain self-control. The adult should have clear reasons for choosing punishment. It is usually more effective to offer an alternative activity that can be positively enforced rather than an intervention that could prove to be a negative reinforcement to a child.

Timing of any punishment should be related to the occurrence of the offense and should not extend over so long a period that it loses meaning for the child.

Group punishment for misbehavior of one or more members is not desirable. It can have the negative long-range effect of embittering the children who are unfairly punished, and may disturb group cohesiveness. The group may become hostile to the individual child, who may feel alone and rejected by them; the group may also direct its hostility to the staff member. Humiliating or degrading punishment, which undermines the child's respect (including ridicule, sarcasm, shaming, scolding, or punishment in the presence of the group or another staff member), should be avoided.

Corporal punishment, including slapping, spanking, paddling, belting, marching, standing or kneeling rigidly in one spot, or any kind of physical discomfort, should not be used. Generally, this is viewed by the child as a manifestation of the adult's aggression rather than punishment, and reinforces any feelings he or she may already have that the world is a hostile, angry, fearful place. For many children, it is a repetition of earlier experiences that have contributed to their problems.

Physical restraint of a child, or interference by an adult in a fight between children, is at times necessary or desirable for the protection of the child or others.

No child should be placed in a locked room without administrative approval. If confinement is necessary in an emergency, a staff person should be in constant attendance upon the child, and the executive director should be advised immediately of the crisis. If confinement is needed for more than one or two hours, there should be an immediate and full evaluation of the appropriateness of the confinement.

3.28 Tutoring

Individual tutoring for all or part of the school day should be arranged for children who need more individual help and instruction than is possible in school.

The center is responsible for providing facilities, equipment, and personnel either in the group living situation or in the school, so that the child can have the additional help and encouragement to make maximum use of school opportunities. Tutoring, however, should be supplementary to school attendance, not a substitute for it.

Health Services

Meeting the health needs of children living in the center requires:

- comprehensive health planning for group living, including a favorable physical and emotional environment; provisions for safety, sanitation, and sanitary food handling; and continuous observation of children and staff to prevent spread of infection

- continued health supervision of individual children
- medical and hospital care for children, as needed

3.29 Responsibility for health program

It is the responsibility of the center to maintain and promote the health of children for whom it assumes responsibility, to prevent illness, to correct defects, and to provide care and treatment for children who are ill. (2.18)

A good health and medical care program requires:

- qualified medical staff, with sufficient time assigned to carry out responsibilities for continuous health supervision and for medical care as soon as any suspicion of illness is noted by staff members
- adequate facilities for physical care
- clearly defined policies and procedures

The health program should be under the technical direction of a physician (preferably a pediatrician, or an internist or general practitioner if children under care are primarily adolescents).

The medical director should be employed as a member of the agency's staff, administratively responsible to the executive director for planning and directing the health services and for coordinating them with the total program.

3.30 Arrangements for health services

Medical, surgical, hospital, and nursing services should be provided by the agency through its own resources or through specific contract with the various medical, dental, and nursing services in the community, including hospitals. (3.40, 3.41–2)

3.31 Admission examination

Each child accepted for care should have a complete physical examination at time of admission or within the first week after admission. (2.11)

The physician making the examination should report his or her observations and findings in writing and in enough detail to show:

- physical condition and state of development
- freedom from or presence of communicable disease
- ability to take part in group activities, or schedule of permitted activities when these must be limited
- recommendations and orders for future care, treatment, and examination

The report of the physical examination should not only be part of the health record but the child's physical status should always be considered in the treatment plan for each child.

The physician in charge should have chief responsibility for carrying out health policies, but they should be developed in conjunction with consultation with other members of the health team, such as the pediatrician, psychiatrist, and staff nurse; a representative of the state or local health department; representatives of the food and housekeeping services and the social work and child care staff; and the executive.

Where there are more than one physician, the medical director should be responsible for supervision and for consultation with them on the medical problems of individual children.

Duties of physicians on the medical staff should include making periodic and other medical examinations, and prescribing, referring, or directing treatment as indicated.

Responsibilities of the different staff members, such as nurse, child care worker, and social worker, in respect to the physical and mental health needs and problems of individual children, and in relation to the health program, should be clearly defined. (2.13)

When there has been insufficient time to prepare a child for placement, and if an adequate medical history can be obtained, the routine physical examination, as well as routine medical procedures, such as immunization, may be postponed.

3.32 Content of admission examination

The initial examination should include:
- health history: developmental history, illnesses and operations, immunizations against common contagious diseases, recent or current use of medicines or drugs
- social, emotional, and environmental history
- health history of family, including social, mental, neurological, and emotional problems
- physical examination, including urine and blood tests, and tests for visual and auditory acuity
- if indicated, neurological examination and psychiatric evaluation
- if indicated, tuberculin test, including chest X-ray
- when especially indicated, blood tests for venereal infection, intestinal parasites, and bacteria; tests that may be disturbing to a child, such as vaginal smears and blood tests for syphilis, are no longer considered necessary as routine procedures

3.33 Immunization

Each child taken into care should be immunized against common contagious diseases, including vaccination for smallpox and immunization against diphtheria, tetanus, poliomyelitis, whooping cough, measles, and rubella.

Initial immunizations and booster injections should be carried out as recommended by the state department of health.

3.34 Periodic examinations

Each child should receive a complete physical examination annually, or at more frequent intervals as recommended by the medical director.

An examination at time of discharge should also be made. A current summary of the child's health record should accompany the child upon transfer to another placement.

At discharge, the child, if old enough, or the caretaker of a younger child, should receive a concise record of medical tests, immunizations, and significant illnesses. This medical "passport" should be considered the child's property.

3.35 Health education

Children should be taught attitudes and habits conducive to health, through daily routines, example, and discussion, and be helped to understand the principles of health and hygiene.

Cleanliness and care of one's body should become an accepted routine. (3.19)

Attention should be given to children with special health conditions.

Children should be helped to understand the importance of proper food and adequate amounts of sleep, rest, play, and exercise, according to their age, physical condition, and physiological and personality characteristics.

3.36 Sex education

Children should be given an accurate and appropriate understanding of sexuality and should be helped to develop desirable standards of sex behavior.

The interest of children in sex should be recognized as an aspect of normal development. They should have an opportunity to discuss their ideas, worries, and concerns about such matters as conception, childbirth, sexual codes and conduct, masturbation, and other facets of family and sexual relationships.

Group or individual discussion among the child care staff, and where appropriate, parents, can help them to be more sensitive to their own attitudes and feelings about sex education and to modes of expression that may differ from their own. Child care staff must be able to answer children's questions in a straightforward way. Pertinent literature, audio-visual materials, and community programs can be made available to children, staff, and when appropriate, parents.

3.37 Medical care

There should be provision for diagnosis and treatment of any physical illness or handicap and for prompt medical care for emergencies and suspected illness. (3.29, 9.58)

It is important for the agency to obtain funds and resources, (i.e., medical, nursing, and hospital care) for diagnosis and treatment of physical illness and handicaps.

Staff members responsible for the care of ill children should receive training in the proper handling and use of medications and in observing and recording a child's reactions to them.

Child care staff should be helped to understand the health problems of children in their care, and to deal with emergency situations, including receiving training in first aid.

3.38 Medication

Treatment or medication should be given only upon order of a physician. When medication is administered, a precise record should be kept of the child's name, the name of the medication, the dosage and time given, and the signature of the person who administers it.

Effects of medication should be noted in the child's health record and the prescribing physician should regularly review the child's response to medication.

When psychotropic medications are used, the reasons should be noted and the response of the child should be logged daily. All staff members should be aware of the side effects of medication prescribed for the child. If medications are used to help a child deal with severe anxiety or depression, daily monitoring of behaviors is essential. The value of the medication must be assessed, as well as the value of the placement, as the child may need more care and protection in a different kind of placement.

Basic medical and hematologic procedures in relation to the use of certain drugs should be carried out according to medical advice.

3.39 Care of sick children

Children who are ill should be cared for in surroundings that are familiar to them, so long as this is medically and socially desirable.

Because children are often frightened and unhappy when isolated, they should not be removed from their group unless absolutely necessary.

A room, or rooms, with bath can be set aside in each cottage and made available for isolation when:
- the child has a contagious or infectious illness
- treatment of minor ailments necessitates quiet for a child, but not hospitalization
- a child who is overtired or overwrought needs to rest

In the event of an epidemic, a living unit can be rearranged to meet the situation.

If isolation rooms are used, staff should always be available to give appropriate care and attention.

The practice of isolating each child on admission to a center, or the use of reception cottages, is no longer considered necessary as routine procedure. A preliminary medical examination is sufficient to indicate whether separation from the group is necessary.

3.40 Hospitalization

Provision should be made and procedures established for hospitalization of children when required, through arrangements with hospitals where good medical care is available.

Construction and equipment of separate hospitals or infirmary buildings as part of a child care residential facility have been found generally unnecessary and impractical. (7.29)

3.41 Health records

A separate health record should be maintained for each child.

The record should contain:

- report of admission physical examination, current medications, if any, and recommendations
- previous and continuing health and medical history, including illness while under care, hospitalization, surgery
- notation of prescribed medicines: the name, date, and expiration date; dosage and time to be administered; and purpose of the medication program
- reports of tests, immunizations, periodic reexaminations, and recommendations
- nursing notes
- reports of psychiatric examinations and psychological tests
- reports of dental examinations and treatment, showing dates and by whom given

A signed parental authorization for medical care, for immunizations, and for hospitalization when indicated, should be on file in the medical record. (2.19)

Health records should be kept in a place where they are readily available to physician and nurse. A periodic summary of the health record should be filed in the case record. (9.30)

3.42 Nursing service

Nursing service should be available and used for:
- care of sick children
- assistance to physician in providing continual health supervision
- interpretation of medical, dental, and nutritional recommendations to staff and children
- followup on medical and dental recommendations (9.60)

As a member of the staff team, the nurse has an important role as consultant to other staff members regarding health needs of individual children, particularly children with physical infirmities or chronic illness, and in contributing to the treatment plan for a child.

The nurse may work directly with children in health education and in discussing concerns about health. She should be able to recognize when these concerns are related to other problems that need to be taken up with other staff members (e.g., social worker, therapist, child care workers, etc.).

3.43 Dental care

The center should arrange for a dental examination as soon as practical after acceptance of the child for care, and for treatment, including necessary prophylaxis, orthodontia, repairs, and extractions when indicated, and for semiannual reexaminations.

> The schedule for examinations, prophylaxis, orthodontia, and other treatment should be planned by the dentist together with medical, social work, and child care staff.

> At time of discharge, the child's current dental record should be made available to the parents, or to the agency responsible for planning for future dental care of the child, or to the older child who is becoming independent.

Mental Health Services

3.44 Psychiatric services

The services of a psychiatrist should be available for diagnosis, consultation, and treatment of a child. (9.61)

> Psychiatric consultation should be available to other staff members working with children in developing a program that promotes mental health and in helping all appropriate staff members understand and use mental health concepts in working with children and their families.

> Use should be made of mental health services and child guidance facilities in the community, whenever they are available, for children and parents.

3.45 Psychological services

The services of a psychologist should be available to contribute to diagnosis and formulation of treatment plans, for direct work with selected children, and for educational and vocational guidance. (9.62)

3.46 Social work services

The services of social workers should be available to contribute to diagnosis, participate in treatment, staff development, and work with the families of the children prior to their admission, when in care, and during aftercare when indicated.

Recreation or Activities Program

Recreation cannot be separated from the total living experience of children. Play is a learning experience as important as formal education. The activities program should further the physical, social, and emotional development of each child. Play and cultural pursuits can also be a part of treatment. Many children, as well as their parents, can be reached through their interests rather than their problems.

In play the child may find courage to express initiative. The first experience of success may be in play, which may then become a step to greater self-confidence and security.

3.47 Spontaneous activities

Provision should be made for free time with little or no staff direction.

Children should have time to be alone and to engage in solitary activities that they enjoy, such as reading; drawing; playing with dolls, puppets, and other toys; working on collections; roller-skating; bicycling. There should be opportunities for group activities to develop spontaneously, such as group singing, dancing, story-telling, listening to records, games. Use of television may have to be governed by rules about hours when viewing is allowed and about choice of programs.

3.48 Planning the recreation program

The recreation program should offer a wide range of indoor and outdoor activities in which participation can be encouraged and motivated, on the basis of individual interests and needs. (9.46)

Recreational activities are those in which children can find pleasure, experience success, and gain confidence.

Exercise promotes health and physical development. When adolescents improve in fitness, their self-concept also improves. Active group play and competitive activities can be balanced by quiet or independent pursuits.

The program should offer organized group activities, such as clubs, sports, and scouting, for children who are ready to participate.

Regimentation, such as mass excursions and program activities imposed on a group, should be avoided.

Activities should be spread throughout the week, and especially on days when there is no school.

Community facilities should be used as much as possible.

3.49 Birthdays and holidays

Observance of birthdays and holidays adds enjoyment to daily living and provides occasions to which children can look forward.

Frequent special events and trips prevent monotony. Varied opportunities contribute to adaptability. In addition, the child care workers' enjoyment of these events reinforces the children's perception of them as actual people—they share the fun, companionship, and adventure. And ceremony and ritual lend a sense of order, stability, and confidence.

Each child's birthday should be celebrated individually in the group living unit.

Ethnic and cultural celebrations are a ready way of honoring diversity among the children.

The agency should avoid having so many activities on special holidays as to preclude the possibility of children planning their own activities with relatives or friends.

3.50 Recreational equipment

Recreational equipment should be selected in accordance with the number of children, their ages and needs, and should allow for imaginative play, creativity, and development of leisure skills and physical fitness.

Equipment owned in common, such as games, should be easily accessible, as well as personal toys, bicycles, sports equipment, and play materials. (7.12)

Religion

Religion in its broadest sense should be a vital part of the life of children in group care, whether they share a common religious background, as in a residential facility under religious auspices, or are of various faiths.

3.51 Participation in religious activities

All children should be given opportunity for religious experiences within the broad religious preferences of their parents. (2.21, 10.4)

The nonsectarian agency has responsibility to provide opportunities for the child who wants to have an appropriate religious affiliation and religious experiences in accordance with the religious preferences of the parents.

The agency under religious auspices, whose religious program is an integral part of its service, should make it clear that its service is so based. Children whose parents want them to make use of such a service should be able to do so. (2.21)

Children and families who do not choose to participate in religious activities should not be expected to do so in any residential center.

The child who has been neglected, who is confused and disturbed, often needs the experiences of faith and acceptance that religion can contribute to the child and family.

Children should be encouraged to participate in religious activities but should not be coerced or expected to participate at times when this would be in conflict with the treatment plan for the particular child. Many children come into group care with conflicts about religious practices, which they should have opportunity to resolve without pressure.

Care should be taken that religious observances do not become so routine that religious activity loses its meaning and becomes simply one more demand of the facility for the child to demonstrate conforming behavior.

Children may become acquainted with religious beliefs and principles through religious literature and songs used in their daily living group, and not only through religious teachers and the clergy, or only on holy days, festivals, or occasions of public worship.

Aspirations, goals, and values can be derived from personal emotional and spiritual experiences, as well as from the religious experiences that are part of the culture into which the child and his or her family were born.

Religious teachings convey an understanding of concepts of right and wrong, and the impact of conscience.

Children should be taught to respect the practices of different faiths and to accept the right to different forms of worship.

3.52 Role of chaplain or pastor

The religious consultant or chaplain should act as a member of the treatment team to help children and their families with their problems and should make use of religious activities selectively in relation to the needs of a particular child and the plan for him or her. (9.65)

The religious consultant can also aid other staff members in understanding the particular meaning of religion in the lives of individual children and families and how social and emotional problems are affected by the staff's attitudes in respect to religion.

3.53 Attendance at community churches

Arrangements should be made for a child to attend a community church of the appropriate faith and to take part in appropriate church activities when it is part of the treatment plan for the child.

At the beginning, it may be necessary for a child care worker to accompany the child until it becomes certain that the child can behave appropriately in the community.

Like other community activities, church attendance in the community may be part of the preparation for leaving the treatment center and moving to the child's own family or other community-based living arrangement.

Participation in the Community

3.54 Community activities

The child should have opportunities to participate in community life when individual treatment has progressed so that community activities can become part of the treatment plan.

The child might participate in activities sponsored by school, church, and national and local youth agencies (Girl Scouts, Boy Scouts, 4-H Clubs, etc.)

In accordance with the treatment plan, a child should be able to visit personal friends in their homes and invite them to the residential facility.

It may be advisable for a child care worker to go with the child to community activities. The child should understand why this is necessary and the child's feelings about it should be protected as much as possible.

Mass excursions, transportation in vehicles labeled with the name of the center, wearing of uniforms, etc., are undesirable if they call attention to the children and make them feel different from others.

The child should have help, when necessary, to conform to community standards.

Children should be encouraged to become acquainted with and develop appreciation for the cultural and educational resources of the community and those particularly relevant to their own interests or cultures, such as places of historical interest, museums, art galleries, ethnic festivals, etc.

Visits to parents and relatives in their own homes should be encouraged, unless they are not of benefit to the child, in order to maintain not only family ties but also ties in the neighborhood and community.

Community interest in children and efforts in their behalf (parties, entertainments, invitations to visit strange families) should be carefully evaluated to ascertain that they are of benefit to the children and do not exploit their dependency status.

Volunteer Program

3.55 Use of volunteers

Volunteers should be used to enrich the program by bringing to it specialized skills and interests not otherwise available to the children through staff, and to offer opportunities for relationships and individualized attention that can be used in the treatment plan for some children. (8.66)

Volunteers represent the interest of the community in the children and in the program.

In addition to their interest, volunteers should have skills that can be used in the program of the center, e.g., in recreation, music, arts, crafts, tutoring, driving, office work, repairing equipment; or qualifications for serving as Big Brothers or Big Sisters for individual children who need them.

For some children, a volunteer can become an important adult model.

Volunteers can make a valuable contribution to the agency by interpreting its program to their friends and to the community.

The center should not plan to use volunteers unless an appropriate staff member can be assigned to select, evaluate, and supervise them and to design a plan for their orientation and training.

The staff person or the administrator should also be responsible for establishing means of formal recognition of volunteers for their contribution to the service.

4

EDUCATION FOR CHILDREN IN A RESIDENTIAL CENTER

Education should be an integral part of the life of children in residential care. The educational plans for a child should be coordinated with the other services to help the child achieve the goals of the treatment plan.

Education of the children in residential facilities has special aspects. The majority of the children have lacked the opportunity or were unable to make the best use of educational opportunities because of family problems, environmental factors, physical and developmental problems, or personality factors. The children's problems may interfere with their motivation for learning or may result in a level of achievement lower than their potential. Special arrangements and facilities are required, including remedial education and tutorial help, to meet individual education needs. (9.63)

Educational Planning and Program

4.1 Responsibility for educational program

A staff member or a director of education should be designated as the individual who is responsible for consultation and planning with other staff members for the education of each child in care; for liaison with community educational services (schools the children attend, special community educational services); for interpretation to staff of the educational factors that affect a child's adjustment and development.

The educational liaison should be a member of the professional staff and have training in education or experience in working with schools and special education programs. If the staff member is a director of education, the training should include a master's degree in special education.

4.2 School attendance

Every child should be helped to achieve the maximum amount of formal education of which he or she is capable, and should be provided the optimum conditions in which to receive the greatest benefits from the school experience. (4.8)

It is the responsibility of the center to see that the children attend school full-time throughout the period required by law, and in general, until the age of 16 years.

Children in care during adolescence should generally be enabled to complete high school. Arrangements for further education or training (college, professional, or vocational) should be made for children whose aptitudes, personalities, and school records show that they can and want to profit from such educational opportunities. (4.9)

For children who have cognitive, emotional, or physical handicaps that prevent them from fully benefiting from regular school programs, pertinent educational services and resources should be provided.

4.3. Educational plan for the child

During the intake, an educational plan should be developed for each child. (2.14)

An educational plan includes:
- the child's present level of performance (2.8)
- annual goals and short-term objectives
- criteria for evaluation
- evaluation procedures
- specific education services
- related services, such as physical therapy, transportation
- the extent to which the child will participate in the regular education program

4.4. Goals of an individual educational plan

The goals of an educational plan should be specific, related to the discharge plan for the child, and based on a thorough assessment of the educational needs of the child by members of the staff and representatives of education who are working with or are responsible for the school program for the child. (2.13)

> Present levels of school performance and other educational data and social behaviors that will be the focus of attention must be clear, so that all members of the team can direct their work to help the child accomplish the educational objectives of the treatment plan.

4.5 Evaluation of educational plan for the child

Within a month of admission, the educational plan for each child should be checked to see that it corresponds with the educational needs of the child.

> At quarterly intervals, generally during the case conferences, the educational plan for each child should be reevaluated and the child's ability to use the educational program should be assessed. (2.15)

> The school experience should also be reviewed to determine the extent of its coordination and integration with other treatment elements for the child, e.g., daily living, social services.

4.6 Participants in educational planning

The staff team, and when appropriate the child, should participate with the school staff and the parents in formulation of the educational plan, and its review and modification. (2.6)

> Care should be taken to ensure that the parents and legal guardians or custodians understand the plans and goals well enough to discuss what is best for the child.

Educational Program

4.7 Use of community school

Children whose academic abilities have not been impaired by their problems or who function adequately academically despite their problems should attend a regular community school. (4.3)

When the child is enrolled in a community school, the school liaison should discuss with the community school teachers the information they need to be able to work most effectively with the child. The center staff must show its willingness to cooperate with the school and its officials in order to find the best ways to motivate individual children to make the best use of educational opportunities.

Child care staff should participate as far as possible in community school activities. They should attend PTA meetings and school functions, particularly when the children participate in them. (5.4)

Facilities should be provided in the child's living unit for quiet study after school hours. Encyclopedias, dictionaries, books, and current magazines should be accessible for homework.

Children able to do so should be encouraged to take part in extracurricular activities.

4.8. Vocational counseling and training

Children of high school age should be prepared for future economic independence.

The school may facilitate work-study programs for children who want to learn how to enter the job market as independent individuals. The school may also facilitate such activities as finding jobs for older children. (3.24, 4.11)

The child should have help both from the school and the social worker or designated center staff member to find a suitable occupation or employment.

Available community facilities should be used for vocational counseling and training if the residential program is not equipped to do so on its own grounds.

4.9 Tutoring for children attending community school

Individual tutoring should be arranged for children who need more individual help and instruction than are provided by the community school.

Children in a residential center may have learning difficulties and be at a disadvantage in relation to the other children in the community school because of frequent change of schools and teachers. They may need special help through social work and remedial education to overcome these difficulties.

In such cases, the residential center is responsible for providing facilities, equipment, and personnel to give the child the additional help and encouragement needed to make maximum use of school opportunities. Tutoring should be a supplement to school attendance, not a substitute for it. (8.20)

Residential Center School

4.10 Center school

A school should be provided on the grounds of the center for children who are functioning below their grade level or who are too disturbed to get along in community schools. (8.20)

Special schools can help children make up for serious retardation and gaps in learning and change their attitude about school experience.

The program should be flexible, with work periods that last only as long as the child can tolerate. Music, arts, and crafts should be used to relieve tension.

Classes should be small enough so that children can have individualized instruction in accordance with different levels of achievement.

The curriculum should be based on knowledge of the possible relationship of learning problems and organic or emotional disturbance.

As individual children progress and make a better adjustment in the agency school, they should be transferred to the community school.

4.11 Coordination of the center school program and center policy

The philosophy of the center, as demonstrated in its policies, should be integrated with the school program. (9.39)

Recognition of the importance of consistency for children requires an identical approach in the school and in group living in such areas as discipline; verbal and nonverbal abuse; recreation; sex education; and confidentiality. The director of education should facilitate transfers to the community school on the basis of the cooperative relations he or she has developed between the center and the community school. (4.3)

4.12 Center school services for children

The school should place its emphasis on the learning needs of each child so that he or she can gain mastery over particular school problems, in learning or behavior or both.

> The program should be flexible, and the classes small enough to provide individualized instruction according to each child's need and level of achievement.

> The school should have qualified teachers, specialists, and resources that meet the requirements of the pertinent educational authorities. The facilities should offer the children special education in their classrooms, with the help of teachers, assistants, aides, equipment, and qualified specialists for particular needs. (4.14)

> The school may also arrange or provide a tutoring program that will help the child prepare for integration in a community school. (3.28)

> Older adolescents in work-study programs or in new jobs can also use the support of school staff. (4.9)

4.13 Aftercare responsibility of the school

Continued support from educational staff should be coordinated with all other aftercare plans of the agency in behalf of the child and family. (2.25)

Educational Administration and Supervision

4.14 The educational administrator

The educational administrator should carry the delegated responsibility for the educational program, supervision of the agency school staff, and consultation with other center staff members on educational matters.

> The administrator is responsible for developing collaboration between the teachers and other staff members so as to contribute to the understanding of and help to the child and family.

> The administrator should have a master's degree in special education and the other school staff members should have the training and certification required by their educational boards.

4.15 Staff development for teachers

Teaching staff should be systematically provided with opportunities for staff development. (9.67)

> An inservice training program for all educational staff members allows for growth and further skill as specialists in the therapeutic education of children with school problems and facilitates the work for and in behalf of the child and family.

> Emphasis should be placed upon training in the theory and practice of collaboration, concepts of child development, group theory, and methods of control, as well as on special techniques to improve pre-academic skills in educationally disadvantaged and neurologically damaged children.

> The training program should include case study approaches, workshops, remedial techniques, and understanding of such creative teaching areas as art, music, and drama.

4.16 Special school facilities

Adequate and proper physical facilities and equipment should be provided in the school. (8.21)

> The design of the school should comply with building codes and should permit educationally determined separation of staff and students of different ages and sexes.

> The design should be such that changes in the size and use of various rooms can be made when population shifts of the children in the center occur.

> The school should have a wide variety of texts, teaching materials, and teaching aids for the teachers to use to encourage individual children. (4.12)

4.17 School records

School records of each child should be maintained by school personnel. (9.29)

> Maintenance of school records should comply with state legislation and regulations of pertinent educational bodies.

5

CHILD CARE IN A RESIDENTIAL CENTER

The child care staff is the heart of the program in a residential facility for children. The degree to which a child can benefit from the total program depends largely on the contribution that the child care worker makes as a member of the staff team carrying out the treatment plan for a particular child.

*Responsibilities of the Child Care Staff**

The child care staff members carry responsibilities for the daily care and supervision of the living group to which each is assigned, and for the individual children in it. The duties may vary in relation to the type of treatment, size, and program of the facility. Under any circumstances, work with the children, individually or as a group, should have precedence over any other duties. The effectiveness with which each child care worker carries out delegated responsibility is directly related to the administrative designation of the number

---

* The term *child care staff* will be used to designate staff members sometimes called house parents, cottage parents, group parents, counselors. It is recognized that there is no generally acceptable term that encompasses the various responsibilities of these staff members in their relationship to the child and family, and that the term used in a given facility derives from its concept of their role. Child care workers include both men and women.

of children in the living group, length of working hours, duties carried other than work with the children, and inservice training and supervision.

5.1 As a team member

The responsibilities of the child care staff should be clearly defined, particularly in relation to the responsibilities of other staff members working with children in the living group. (1.8)

The child care staff as treatment team members should take part in discussions of plans for, and progress of, individual children in her or his group, and in decisions regarding intake, grouping, future treatment, discharge, etc. (2.10, 2.13–2.15, 2.24, 2.25, 3.2, 4.8).

They should contribute to and receive information about the treatment and future plans for the child and family so that treatment proceeds in an integrated fashion.

The child care staff should know whom to consult about specific problems or situations: the person who has administrative responsibility or the member of the professional staff who has responsibility for a particular child.

Provision should be made for conferences and staff meetings to ensure regular communication with the staff team and also with the other child care staff members concerned with the daily life of the children. (9.19)

5.2 Child-rearing responsibilities

The child care worker should be clearly designated as the person in charge of the living group and should carry the child-rearing responsibilities that parents usually perform. (3.14–3.28)

In the living group, child care staff make it possible for the child to have some of the experiences and relationships that children ordinarily have in families.

Many of the child's or adolescent's dependency needs must be met, such as being cared for and protected, and at the same time, each child must be helped to become increasingly independent and able to assume appropriate responsibilities.

Child-rearing responsibilities include:

Physical care: Seeing to it that food, meals, and snacks are provided;

creating a pleasant atmosphere at mealtime, and eating with the children; seeing that the children have enough sleep and rest; caring for and comforting a sick child; maintaining a reasonably clean and orderly place for the children to live. (3.14–3.19, 5.9)

Development of habits: Helping the child meet social expectations that are appropriate for his or her age and developmental level; e.g., cleanliness, eating habits, toilet habits, care of personal appearance, sex hygiene, manners, accepted modes of social living, routines, rules, and procedures. (3.16–3.19)

Care of clothing: Seeing that the child has and wears suitable clothing in good condition. (3.20)

Teaching management of money: Helping the child learn the appropriate use of money and giving the child his or her allowance. (3.22)

Assignment of daily and weekly chores: Planning, discussing, and making work assignments. (3.23)

Help with schoolwork: Particularly when requested by the child. (3.28)

Teaching values: Ethical principles, religious observances, moral development. (3.51)

Discipline: Helping the child learn, and act with, responsibility. (5.6)

5.3 Individualization of the child in the group

The child care worker should treat each child as an individual, different from other children, and should modify his or her role according to each child's particular needs and the center's treatment plan. (1.8)

Child care workers must recognize that a child regards each one of them as individuals and relates to each staff member in a different way.

The child care worker must help each child to find acceptance and status in the group and should see to it that a child does not get lost in his or her group. A child care worker can help a child develop self-restraint and self-esteem from repeated successes, concrete achievements, and approval.

To be able to individualize children and to be understanding of and responsive to each child and his or her needs, a child care worker can be responsible only for a limited group of children at a time.

The kind and degree of disturbances or handicaps that each child has should be considered by the administration in the assignment of responsibility to each child care staff member.

5.4 Role in treatment of a child's problems

In carrying out the plan for each child, the child care worker should coordinate his or her role with the roles of other team members with whom they share responsibility. (2.14)

Each child care staff member has the responsibility of helping the child to have daily living experiences in the group that are growth promoting and that counteract previous unsatisfactory experiences that have affected the child's behavior.

The relationship between a child and the child care worker is a crucial aspect of the total treatment program. The child care staff is responsible for the development of defined standards of living and for the children's adherence to them.

The child care worker should be responsible primarily for dealing with the child's behavior and feelings as they are related to the current reality and in situations of daily living. There may be a need to take action on the spot in regard to expressions of the child's own problems that are unacceptable in a group, or to allow the child to express feelings by listening sympathetically and with understanding. The child can be helped to understand that full discussion of problems is a more constructive means of handling problems than impulsive and destructive acts.

The child care worker should know about the child's problems so that he or she can help the child manage individual reactions to reality situations. This information is generally communicated in team planning for the child.

In turn, the child care worker reports observations of significant behavior to other staff members in treatment conferences, or in emergencies to the staff member who carries treatment responsibility for a child. Informal conferences should never take the place of regular treatment-planning conferences.

5.5 Providing group living experiences

The child care staff should make it possible for the children in their care to have positive group living experiences.

It is necessary to plan for group living and not to try to create a pseudofamily. Perhaps the most important means of creating cohesion in the living situation is the group meeting. One of its several values is bringing together all of the youngsters for a positive learning experience in group interaction.

In addition, group routines can be used imaginatively and purposefully to give children security in the group, to enable them to learn how to relate to others in a socially acceptable way, to help them understand the need for required routines and procedures and then accept and conform to them.

Child care staff can help children feel that they are part of the group, living and belonging together, and foster tolerance and acceptance of one another.

Each child care worker should be aware of the interaction of children in the group, with each other and with the adults, and be able to make use of such group processes as identification, participation, and leadership to achieve social and educational goals.

The leadership potentials of individual children must be recognized.

The group living experience should provide for recreational experiences and periods of fun.

5.6 Responsibility for discipline

The child care worker should be the person in authority for the group and should have the responsibility for discipline of the children in the living unit in accordance with an administratively defined approach to discipline, controls, and punishment (3.15, 3.25–3.27).

> The child care worker represents adult authority to the children in the group and is in a position to give, share, and withhold. The child care worker must feel comfortable in the role of authority.

> Child care workers should have a part in deciding the methods of discipline that are and are not acceptable within the limits of center policy. The center should provide inservice training in approved discipline procedures. (9.39)

> The child care staff member should arrange with the administratively responsible staff member for consultation when necessary about individual children or group situations. The administrative staff member should initiate consultation whenever there appears to be improper, excessive, or insufficient use of discipline.

5.7 Participation in recreational activities

The child care worker should encourage the group to participate in activities and pleasurable events in the living units, in the recreation program, and in the community, and should take part with the children in games, sports, parties, outings, and quiet play activities.

> In consultation with the recreation director, plans for activities for children in the living unit should be geared to individual and group interests. (3.48)

> It is not always necessary to participate actively in the children's play in the living unit, but children should have the feeling that the child care staff is interested in their recreation.

> Suitable materials for the children should be available in the living unit, such as paper, paints, books, and records, and the children should be encouraged to use them.

5.8 Observation of children

Each child care worker should be responsible for observing the functioning and development of individual children in the group, for being aware of difficulties related to the group or to their family situations, and for recording significant information about each child at regular intervals. (9.29–9.31)

> This may be done by keeping a daily log and by preparing summaries periodically, as required for staff meetings and joint planning in treatment conferences. The log is especially useful in communicating daily happenings and problems from one shift of workers to another.

> This information should be made available to all staff members responsible for working directly with individual children and their families and for evaluating a child's progress.

> The purpose of records should be clearly defined: for understanding and working with individual children, for supervision of child care staff, or for inservice training.

> Inservice training for child care workers should foster development of their skills in observation of significant aspects of individual and group behavior.

> The daily schedule should allow sufficient time each day for recording.

5.9 Housekeeping

The child care worker should be responsible for management of the group living unit and for seeing that maintenance requirements are met, but should not ordinarily be required to carry out all the household duties.

He or she may supervise preparation and serving of food, as well as cleaning—both general tidiness and heavy cleaning, laundry and clothing maintenance, etc. Child care workers, however, should not be involved in duties that leave the children unattended, e.g., cooking.

Some household chores may be assigned to the children so that they can share the aspect of group living that includes routine assignments and responsibility for their home. The best way to teach a child to work is to work along with the child, showing him or her what to do and how to do it. (3.23)

5.10 Relationship to child's parents

Child care staff should make parents feel comfortable and accepted when they visit.

In contacts with parents, and in talking with them or listening to the child, the child care worker should convey respect and understanding of the importance of the parents to the child. Child care staff, recognizing what the parents mean to a child, should control their disapproval or criticism if the parents disappoint or upset a child, and avoid showing resentment to the child or parents.

The parents should be encouraged to carry such responsibilities for the child as they can and as are part of the plan.

The child care worker's observations of the parent-child relationship should be included in the daily log and periodic summaries for the treatment team.

6

SOCIAL WORK IN A RESIDENTIAL CENTER

Social work services with the child and parents, beginning with the intake study and continuing throughout the period of placement to discharge and aftercare, are an essential part of the total service in the residential center. Social work services should be closely related to the group living program and other services within and outside of the center. Social work, including both individual and group methods, is the key service of residential care. The social worker has a key role in planning and coordination of all services to the child and family.

6.1 Use of social work services

Social work services should constitute a method of helping the child and parents with their particular needs in order to bring about improvement in the social and emotional problems necessitating residential care. It is a method of direct treatment for problems in social functioning.

Social work services should be used

- to help determine if there is a need for residential service (2.2–2.6, 5.3)
- to obtain and coordinate pertinent social information from various sources, as needed (6.2)
- to help ensure that the resources of the residential facility are

being used according to the treatment plan, in daily living, school, health, recreation, religious and community activities, and in the family situation (2.10)

- to help the child and family directly with those problems that necessitated residential care and those associated with the separation and placement that can be best helped through the social work relationship, through individual and family interviews and/or through group meetings and services (5.8)
- to help parents with particular problems affecting their relationship with their child, their ability to carry parental responsibilities, and their capacity to establish or reestablish their home with the child
- to help the parents and their child with plans for discharge and aftercare services (6.10, 6.14)

Responsibilities of the Social Worker

6.2 As a team member

The social worker should be a member of the staff team working with individual children and should participate in planning and carrying out all phases of the plan for each child, from intake to discharge (2.10, 2.13–2.15, 6.7)

The social worker should contribute pertinent information to other staff members about the situation of the child and family including:

- information about the child's family background, past experiences, and problems that affect the child's responses in present situations
- significant occurrences throughout the child's placement, e.g., changes in the family situation, community activities
- special circumstances connected with visits, vacations
- changes in social or legal relationships of the child and parents

The social worker should see that special services are initiated as needed and that arrangements are made for physical examinations, school transfers, liaison with the court, etc.

The social worker must work in close cooperation with all members of the staff team, and with other individuals or agencies that have a significant relationship to the child. (2.9)

6.3 For the intake study

It is the responsibility of the social worker to study and evaluate the problems and needs of the child and parents in order to help the parents arrive at a decision as to whether residential care or some other service is appropriate. (2.7–2.11)

Basic work with the parents focuses on an evaluation of whether the home can be maintained for the child. (2.17, 2.23)

Recognition of ethnicity and cultural differences is important in this study. An awareness of ethnic and cultural values, internal stresses, and extent of acculturation is essential for appropriate evaluation and planning. (1.5) The social worker should help the child participate in the intake process and the final decision that residential service is appropriate. The extent and kind of participation will be determined by the child's age, maturity, the nature of family relationships, and the circumstances necessitating placement. In the contacts with the child, the social worker should seek to learn the child's understanding of what is happening and the child's feelings about it. (1.5)

6.4 Referrals

If necessary, the social worker should help parents accept referral to a needed service, make the practical arrangements, and obtain the service. The social worker should follow up to see that the parents are able to use the other resource. (2.11, 2.26)

Social Work with the Child

6.5 Relationship of the social worker to the child

At intake, a social worker should be assigned to each child and remain for a continuing relationship until the child no longer needs the service of the agency.

The relationship with the social worker should help the child bridge the gap between living at home and the present surroundings, and should continue throughout the period of placement and discharge.

The social worker should begin to develop a relationship with the child during intake.

The relationship of the child with the social worker should be discussed both with the child and the family.

The child should have close contact with the social worker while putting down roots in the new situation.

During stress situations, such as a long period between visits with the family, hospitalization, or other disturbing experiences, special help may also be advisable.

Special attention should be given to changes affecting the relationship of the child with the social worker and other staff members, such as changes in frequency of contact with the parents or the worker, transfer of the worker, or staff vacation absences, that may remind the child of other difficult separation and change experiences and result in behavioral upsets. The child should have adequate preparation for changes and help in understanding the reasons. Social work should be used to prevent unnecessary stress and resultant problems, as well as to alleviate problems.

6.6 Preparation of the child for placement

The social worker should be responsible for helping the parents prepare the child for placement, if this is possible, and for discussion of the planned move so that the child understands the reasons for it and for the selection of residential care. The more the parents can be helped to take responsibility for preparations, the easier it is for the child to accept the placement. (2.12, 2.17)

Before placement occurs, the social worker should encourage the child to express feelings and thoughts about the placement and to relate to staff members such as child care workers, who will be working with the child and family during the placement.

The social worker should acknowledge the child's feelings about his or her parents, both positive and negative, and assist the child to develop an objective attitude toward them.

It is important for the social worker to acknowledge the child's and the parents' feelings and thoughts about the placement, both positive and negative.

The period of preparation should be long enough for the child to have several interviews with the social worker and other staff members.

6.7 Social work with the child during placement

Throughout the placement, the social worker should be a part of the staff team that is responsible for providing direct help to the child in accepting residential care and in making the best possible use of the group living experience. (6.2)

The social worker can help the child:

- face feelings about placement
- understand why it is necessary to live away from the family
- resolve, insofar as possible, confusion and conflict about having to live away from home
- recognize the limitations of the family situation
- recognize that living apart from the family will result in having to learn to live with them again or in another family or placement
- recognize and accept conflicting loyalties
- understand the plan that has been made and the changes that occur in the plan, so that the child can participate more easily and constructively in the plan for discharge (e.g., decision to return home, an independent living arrangement, adoption, placement with a foster family or in a group home) (2.6, 2.13–2.15)
- understand the roles of the various staff members working with him or her
- facilitate constructive use of the available environment and relationships

The social worker may at times have to support authoritative decisions and help the child face unalterable situations and requirements.

6.8 Social work treatment of problems

As determined by the treatment plan, the social worker may provide direct treatment for children with problems in social functioning due to emotional conflicts.

In the treatment of such children, the social worker must have appropriate training (generally postgraduate training) as a therapist, or consultation with a psychiatrist, mental health professional, or social worker with both the requisite training and significant years of experience. (3.44, 3.46)

The social worker can help the child to understand feelings and behavior with respect to relationships; mixed feelings about separations and losses; feelings of rejection and rivalry with siblings; feelings of inadequacy, insecurity, and anxiety.

In family therapy, the social worker helps the child and family to recognize what their behavior means to each other, to evaluate realistically how their behavior may be judged by others, to consider the consequences it brings about, and to assume some responsibility for changing it. (3.11)

6.9 Frequency of interviews

Frequency and intensity of interviews should be related to the treatment plan as determined by the individual needs or problems of each child. (2.13–2.15)

> At the beginning of placement, there may be regular appointments scheduled for discussion of the child's adjustment and any initial problems. Most children need more interviews both at this time and during preparation for departure from the center to deal with the change.

> Children with serious behavior disorders and internalized problems often require more frequent contact and at times the use of professional consultation, e.g., psychiatric, neurological, etc.

6.10 Preparation for termination

The social worker should work directly with the child who is preparing for a return to the community and has to consider day-to-day living, school placement, vocational counseling, job finding, and continuing social work and mental health services.

> The child should have an opportunity to face and resolve feelings about leaving the residential facility, the staff, and the other children.

> If the child will not be returning to the parents, considerable time must be allowed to make and implement the appropriate plan for the child after discharge from care and to assist the child in understanding and accepting the plan.

> If the child is to return home, the social worker should see to it that the child and the family as a whole make an orderly plan for the move and for needed services at home.

> The social worker has more extensive responsibilities when the child will be placed with a foster or adoptive family, in a group residence, or with another social agency. (2.26)

Social Work with Parents

> The family should be involved and participate in all stages of the child's placement, beginning at intake, and should at all times take into account how the decision was made for the child's placement.

> Throughout the period of placement, parents should have con-

tinuing help to maintain a relationship with their child, to take as much responsibility as they can in planning for their child, to work closely with the agency, and to prepare for the child's return to the family or for another arrangement when necessary or preferable.

6.11 Continuing work with the parents

The social worker should arrange for regular interviews with the parents to discuss with them their child's needs, how they see the child developing, adjusting, and using the group living experience, and the parents' plan for the child and themselves.

The parents may need help in accepting the conditions of placement, particularly when their rights are limited; in understanding the program and procedures of the center; in understanding the agency's responsibility and their own; and in clarifying the roles of the various staff members who work with the child. Specific areas include:

- clarification of their relationship to the child and to other agencies and organizations, for example, the agency that assumes financial responsibility for the child, the court or other designated group that reviews periodically the child's continuing need for placement or for another plan, etc.
- the place and frequency of visits and the scheduling of time in relation to the child's needs and the parents' situation
- the extent of their responsibility for continued relationship with the child

The social worker must help the parents plan and manage visits, and especially so when the child has lived elsewhere and when permanent separation is the ultimate plan.

Parents should know that the social worker is interested in what is happening in the family and the effects on the child, e.g., changes in marital status, new children in the family, how the parents are getting along together without the child, how home visits go, and the effects of the visits for their child and themselves and other family members.

The social worker should ensure parental participation in decisions about placement, visiting, and discharge planning. (2.6, 2.12–2.23)

6.12 Social work with the parents

The social worker should provide help to parents with problems that affect their relationship with the child and their ability to carry parental responsibilities or establish a home for the child. (2.14, 3.46)

No matter how calm the parents seem during the initial planning for the child's entry into care, the separation creates conflicted emotions. Whether the parents have requested service or are referred by the court, the social worker should continually evaluate their capacity for and interest in functioning as parents and help them to strengthen, maintain, or terminate the child/parent relationship as determined to be in the best interests of the child. The parents are persons with rights, strengths, values, and needs of their own. Support and help offered to them must convey respect and a realistic view of their present abilities during the placement and afterwards, when tensions generated by readjustment can be severe enough to impede new adaptations by the child and family.

The social worker should make available the help needed for the family to deal more effectively with environmental or emotional stresses that impair parental functioning or contribute to the child's problems, and with the added conflict and stress that may arise in reaction to placement of the child.

The parents may also need or want help to modify feelings and attitudes about themselves, their child, or each other, so that they can foster the child's healthy development. Individually or in groups, such help can be a significant means of helping parents to be more comfortable and effective.

6.13 Social work in relinquishment

The parents should be helped by the social worker to relinquish the child when this is the necessary or desirable way to achieve a permanent plan for the child. (2.18, 9.24)

The social worker should offer support and assistance to the parents and interpret the meaning and process of termination of their rights. The social worker should help the parents to handle the approaching termination as well as they can with the child and to diminish their visits to the child.

If the parent is not the legal guardian, the agency will need to inform the legal guardian or the court about the parental situation. The social worker should tell this to the parents and let them know what recommendations have been made.

6.14 Preparation of parents for the child's discharge from the center

The social worker should help parents plan for and be prepared for the child's discharge from the center, for return home or another living arrangement. (2.25)

> Parents may need help in understanding that a child who has lived apart from them for a while may have mixed feelings about returning home, particularly if the child has made a successful adjustment at the center.

> If the parents have not maintained a continuing relationship with the child, they will need help to reestablish a relationship with the child before the placement is terminated.

6.15 Social work after discharge

Social work services should be available after the child returns home, during the period of readjustment of the child, parents, and other family members to each other. (2.26)

> When the parents or the child need or want further help, continuation of service in their own home should be provided by the agency, or referral should be made to the appropriate service of the same or another agency.

Case Records

6.16 Responsibility for case record

The social worker should be responsible for keeping a continuing record of the service provided for the child and parents. (2.15, 9.29, 9.30)

> The case record should be kept in one place and used in planning for each child and should assure continuity of service when there are staff changes or shifts in the program for the child.

> The case record should include pertinent information necessary for:
> - understanding and evaluating needs and problems of the child and the family, and their capacities for dealing with them
> - continuing evaluation of the child's development, functioning, and progress, and any appropriate revision of the plan
> - evaluating the quality and quantity of service

6.17 Confidentiality of case record

Information obtained by the social worker during intake and placement that contributes to the understanding, care, and treatment of the child and the parents, or that is required for the child's health or safety or the safety of others, should be communicated to and available to other appropriate staff members. (9.13)

> Review and communication of case material is a continuing process. It is essential in planning and delivery of service to the child and family. It presupposes the responsible and professional use of case material by each staff member involved.
>
> The children and their families need to know about the policies as well as legislation, regulations, and funding bodies that require disclosure of personal information. Ordinarily, any decision to release personal information requires the consent of the parent and/or the older child. Exceptions to this principle should be discussed with them so that they understand the conditions for using the service. Many issues concerning agency responsibility to provide confidentiality are under governmental and judicial review. As one aspect of its disclosure policy, the agency should evaluate any request for personal information, the likelihood of maintenance of confidentiality by a third party, and the pertinence of the requested information.

7

GROUPWORK IN A RESIDENTIAL CENTER

The most distinctive feature of life in a residential setting is the involvement of children and staff in a variety of groups and group living situations. Most of the staff members find themselves at one time or another in a group leadership role or close to some phase of the group life of children.

7.1 Use of groupwork

The groupworker has specialized knowledge and skills acquired in graduate study and practice. The skills of the groupworker should be used to enable administrative and other staff members to plan and use the various forms of group experience within the residential facility for the care and treatment of individual children, and to provide direct help in their treatment of children in small, purposefully planned groups. (0.17, 3.2)

Groupwork can help the individual child obtain the maximum benefit from group living experiences. (0.4, 0.8, 0.9)

The groupworker, in addition to a basic knowledge of social work, has distinctive knowledge and skills:

- indepth knowledge regarding group process and its relationship to individual dynamics
- specific skill in being a helping person to members of a group and in developing relationships among members of a group

- understanding of nonverbal behavior
- knowledge of and skill in differential use of programs and in relating a variety of group experiences to the needs of both the individual child and the group

Responsibilities of the Groupworker

7.2 As a team worker

The groupworker should be a member of the staff team working with individual children and should participate in planning and carrying out all phases of the plan for each child, from intake to discharge. (2.6, 2.9, 2.11)

The groupworker attends all case conferences about each child. (9.19)

7.3 Participation of groupworker in intake

At intake the groupworker should take part in the decision as to whether the child should be accepted for care. (2.6)

The groupworker should learn about the child from the intake material, observation of the child if possible, and from participation in the intake conference.

The groupworker should help assess the capacity of the child for group living and for placement in a particular group.

7.4 Responsibility for grouping

The groupworker should take part in determining in which living group the child should be placed, and assist in integrating the child into the group. (3.3)

The groupworker's understanding of the group process in the different living groups should be the basis for recommending the group that is most suitable for a given child.

The groupworker should be responsible for the preparation of child care staff and other children in the group so that they can accept the new child and help him or her have a positive group experience.

7.5 Participation in evaluation and planning

In evaluating progress of the individual children and planning for them, the groupworker should contribute observations and understanding of the child's relationships in various groups and the impact of groups and social processes on him or her, and make recommendations regarding new or different group experiences as the child's needs change. (2.9, 2.11)

Observations of the child's functioning in group and interview situations with an adult are important in evaluating the child's social and emotional development and in planning further treatment.

7.6 Groupwork with children

The groupworker should be responsible for planning and providing experiences in small activity or discussion groups for children who can be helped to deal with their problems through interpersonal relationships and the group process. (3.10, 3.11)

Specially formed groups may be used to help children become adjusted to living in the center and to cope with the realities of life as members of society:

Newcomer groups: The groupworker gives the children the opportunity to discuss freely their anxieties and expectations and to have a relationship with an adult whom they must share with others but who gives them a high degree of individual attention. The groupworker supplies information about the center and helps them with their relationships with both staff members and children.

Group living councils: The groupworker helps children express their dissatisfactions, find satisfaction in being heard and in participating responsibly in certain discussions, and in assuming some responsibility for the life of their community.

Preparation for discharge groups: The groupworker helps children face realistically the problems of moving out of the protected environment of the center through discussion with one another and through role playing and planned activities that allow the child to experience the new environment in advance.

Treatment groups: The groupworker helps children in a group to talk about their problems, act them out, or both. The groupworker may help certain children, when indicated in the treatment plan, with the same problems as the social worker does, but in the treatment group. Psychiatric consultation should be available to the groupworker for the treatment groups. (3.11)

7.7 Work with parent discussion groups

The groupworker may carry responsibility for the composition of the parent groups and for direct work with them.

The groupworker has skills that can help parents, through group discussion, share their concerns about their children, understand the responsibility of the center, and prepare for the discharge of their child.

The groupworker can help parents in treatment groups through discussion of handling of children and their problems. This may be in relation to discipline, school attendance, various habits, etc.

7.8 Groupwork records

The groupworker should be responsible for maintaining continuing records of group sessions and making them available to other staff members involved with the children and parents to whom they refer.

Confidentiality of groupwork records, as of all professional records, must be protected. (9.28)

7.9 Supervision of child care staff

The groupworker may be assigned responsibility for supervision of child care staff. (8.37)

The groupworker should help child care workers make practical use of the principles of group dynamics in everyday situations, and understand the impact on individual children of peer and adult-child relationships in the group. (5.4)

The group worker should help the child care worker develop a rich and individualized program for his or her group, and feel comfortable in the group leadership role. (5.6, 5.7)

7.10 Consultation with recreation staff

The groupworker should serve as a consultant to the recreational staff in relation to understanding the group process. (3.47–3.50)

Recreational staff members have their own competence, but can benefit by consultation regarding operation of the group process in their particular activity group and its impact on particular individuals.

7.11 Consultation with volunteer group leaders

The groupworker should serve as a consultant to volunteer group leaders, and may carry responsibility for the volunteer program. (3.55, 8.64)

The groupworker should be responsible for inservice training of volunteers and differentiating the role of the volunteer from that of staff members.

The groupworker may be responsible for recruiting volunteers or be of help by interpreting the services of the center.

The groupworker who is responsible for all volunteers should share responsibility with social workers who have relationships with volunteers who work only with individual children.

Relationships with Other Staff Members

The functions of the groupworkers must be both closely interrelated with and differentiated from those of other staff members, particularly child care workers, social workers, recreational workers, teachers, and psychotherapists.

7.12 Relationship of groupworker and social worker

The groupworker and the social worker must work closely together in planning and setting goals for individual children and in exchanging information that will help the child.

As members of the same profession sharing a common body of knowledge, groupworkers and social workers may be able to take responsibility for some of the same areas of the residential service. (2.9)

Each will carry out his or her role through the method in which he or she is most competent. Depending, however, on the size of the center and the number of children and staff members, either one may be called upon to develop competence in using both methods. (2.10, 2.12)

7.13 Relationship of groupworker and recreation worker

The role of the groupworker should be differentiated, in particular, from that of the recreation worker in respect to their use of the group program.

The groupworker has a goal of improved social functioning for the individual members of the group and plans the group program according to the assessment of their individual needs, consciously helping the members of the group to use various group relationships and activities to solve social problems and to develop healthier personalities.

The recreation worker places major emphasis on the program itself, in order to help the group members develop healthier personalities by enjoying themselves and gaining new skills from the activities.

8

PLANT AND EQUIPMENT

Needs of children and modern concepts of their social treatment, rather than any particular style of architecture, should be the basis for the building plan of a residential facility. It should not be expected to duplicate a family home, but should be designed to create a warm, attractive, homelike atmosphere for daily living and to provide for the treatment of the child. To be avoided is a cold, depersonalized appearance, complicated layouts, and unnatural scattering of the activities of children's everyday life.

8.1 Building plans

Buildings and grounds should be arranged to make best use of the elements in group living and to bring them together so that the child's daily living experiences may be unified, harmonious, and intimate to the greatest extent possible.

Construction and arrangement of buildings should combine daily living and leisure activities within separate small physical units. From the point of view of the children, unit services rather than central services and facilities are preferable. (3.2, 3.4, 3.12, 8.22)

Such factors as age of children, behavior problems, and physical disabilities should be taken into account in determining variations in space requirements, arrangement of physical facilities, equipment, etc., to ensure accessibility inside and outside the building. (3.13)

The following generalizations should be observed in planning a residential facility:

- In planning new buildings, it should be recognized from past experience that they may serve their present purpose for no more than 20 years. Expansion, convertibility of space, and versatility should be considered for most buildings.
- Buildings should be well constructed, durable, attractive, and functional in design.
- The plan should provide for comfort, convenience, and easy maintenance, as well as minimum effort in staff supervision of children inside buildings and on the grounds.
- The special needs of handicapped children and adults should be considered in planning doorways, halls, placement of windows, etc.
- One-story buildings facilitate supervision, reduce fire hazard, and eliminate stair climbing.
- Choice of color for walls and other units should take into consideration the importance of color for children. A well-qualified and practical interior decorator can assure effective use of materials, colors, and design. In renovation, the children's wishes should be considered in the selection of color.

8.2 Location

Location should be determined by accessibility to public transportation, which is essential for the families of the children and the staff, and availability of hospitals, clinics, psychiatric services, churches, libraries, recreational and cultural facilities. Public schools should also be available if any of the children will be attending them.

A location on the outskirts of a city helps to some extent in solving the problem of attracting and keeping staff who do not wish to be deprived of community contacts by living in a remote rural area. The quality of the school system should be a paramount consideration. (4.8)

The socioeconomic background of children in the community and those accepted for care should not be widely disparate.

8.3 Grounds

The grounds should be attractive, with lawn, shade trees, and flowers, and should afford sufficient space for outdoor activities. (8.20)

Grounds should be maintained for the children's use, not solely for display.

8.4 Maintenance

A maintenance plan with budgetary provision is necessary to ensure keeping plant, grounds, and equipment in good condition. (9.48)

8.5 Building access

The agency should examine its existing buildings to determine the need for changes to ensure access by the handicapped to its program of services; the design of new buildings should be barrier-free.

Basic categories to check include doors, windows, furnishings, floors, halls, equipment and controls, water fountains, bathrooms, rest rooms, and telephones.

When undertaking any building program, the following steps are necessary:

- The board of directors should determine how much money will be available for the project and commission an architect of recognized standing to design the project within the budgetary limit. The board, together with the staff, should be responsible for preparing a building program for the facility. The architect can help them in doing so, particularly in keeping it within the budget, but should not undertake to do so alone.
- After the program has been prepared, the executive and the chairman of the building committee of the board should consult with the architect as preliminary plans are developed, to decide on workable solutions to the problems the program presents. The practical experience of executive, child care staff, dietitian, recreation staff, social workers, psychiatrist, and physician should be taken into consideration.
- Plans should be reviewed by the building committee when they reach the preliminary stage and before they are approved by the board. The state department responsible for licensing children's services and appropriate national standard-setting agencies should be asked to review and advise on plans. Local commissioners, e.g., for zoning and building, and departments, e.g., fire and health,

can help with the early stages of building or renovation to assure conformance with building codes and with special requirements such as the avoidance or removal of physical obstacles that can cause problems to handicapped children and adults.

Living Units

8.6 Arrangement of living units

Construction and arrangement of the building should enable each living group and the child care workers assigned to it to be housed in a unit containing all the rooms required to meet their living needs. (3.2, 3.4, 8.17)

A well-arranged, carefully planned living unit makes it easy and natural for the group to assemble with child care workers at various times during the day. The opportunity to do so within familiar personal confines gives children a feeling of having a place of their own and a group to which they belong.

The children's bedrooms, bathrooms, play space, study areas, living rooms, dining room, and kitchen should be conveniently grouped and close to each other.

A unit may be one of several in one building or may be a separate cottage.

8.7 Bedrooms

The number of bedrooms should be based on their accommodating from one to two children each.

No more than two children should ever occupy one room, so that the individual needs of each child in the group can be met and each child can feel that he or she has a room to enjoy privacy alone or with a few friends.

At least one-third of the bedrooms should be single rooms for children who specially need them, regardless of the age of the children served by the center. Adolescent groups, however, should have more single rooms than younger groups of children. (3.18)

Cubic space of bedrooms should at least meet state and health standards, but it is recommended that each bedroom, including single rooms, should have no less than 700 cubic feet of space per child. Beds should be 3 feet apart on all sides.

All sleeping rooms should be outside rooms, well ventilated, adequately lighted, and heated. Walls should be painted and washable, with provision for children to mount pictures (e.g., peg board, cork strips). Floors should be warm and easily cleaned.

8.8 Beds

Each child should have a separate bed, equipped with level springs, a clean, comfortable mattress, bedding appropriate for weather and climate, and plastic mattress cover or other protection from bed-wetting, if necessary.

8.9 Bedroom furnishings

Each child should have at least an individual chest of drawers, a table or desk, an individual closet with clothes racks and shelves within easy reach, and a place for personal play equipment. (3.20, 3.21)

Each room should have a good mirror. Adolescent girls need a dressing table or a table to use as one.

8.10 Bath and toilet facilities

There should be a sufficient number of separate toilet and bathing facilities for boys, girls, and staff, with a ratio of at least one toilet, bathtub or shower, and washbasin for four children, with provision for privacy.

Toilet facilities should be convenient to sleeping, living, and recreation rooms.

Each child should have a place to keep toothbrush and personal towel and washcloth in the bathroom.

When stall showers are used, there should be at least one bathtub available.

There should be an adequate supply of hot and cold water at all times.

8.11 Living room

Each unit should include a living room where children can gather at any time, for quiet reading and study, general relaxation, or entertaining.

The living room should be a cozy, attractive, inviting place in which the children can take pride.

Books, magazines and newspapers, television, record player, radio, plants, and flowers help to create a homelike atmosphere.

Curtains, rugs, pictures, and other accessories should be chosen with the children's participation, when feasible, and with their interests in mind.

8.12 Indoor play space and equipment

In addition to the living room, there should be well-lighted and ventilated play space adapted to the specific needs of the children in each unit.

Space should be arranged for active play and games, in addition to a place and equipment for table games and individual hobbies.

Books, magazines, and arts and crafts materials should be suited to the children's cultural interests and educational needs.

Shelves and storage space for toys and equipment that all the children can use should be arranged to make them readily accessible.

8.13 Dining area

A dining area should be arranged and equipped so that children can have their meals in their own living unit, and mealtime can be an enjoyable experience. (3.17, 8.6)

Walls and floors should be of attractive and easy-to-clean materials.

Attractive dishes, silverware, placemats or tablecloths, and napkins should be provided to add dignity and beauty to mealtimes, and to encourage children to develop orderly living habits and manners.

If a central dining room has to be used, it should be arranged so that each group of children and their child care worker can have a section where they can eat together in small groups.

8.14 Kitchen

Regardless of the plan for preparation and serving of food, each living unit should have a well-equipped modern kitchen with a stove, sink, refrigerator, dishwasher, garbage-disposal unit (where permitted), and storage space for snacks and other supplies. (8.23)

Unit kitchens have the advantage of allowing food preparation that takes into consideration individual tastes of children. It is possible to centralize preparation of food and transport it to the living units in heated carts.

When food is prepared centrally, there should also be kitchen facilities in each living unit for serving snacks, and recreational activities such as making popcorn or candy, baking, etc. It is possible to have breakfasts and Sunday night supper prepared in the living unit, with the children assisting and having an opportunity to express their individual tastes.

Colors, washable wallpaper, and other decorative amenities should be used to make the kitchen homelike and inviting.

8.15 Utility room

A comfortable, well-lighted and ventilated utility room should be provided in each living unit.

It should be equipped with sewing supplies, a sewing machine, a table, a mirror, and lockers.

Whether or not there is a central laundry, each living unit should have a washing machine and dryer, an iron and ironing board, and other equipment for suitable care of personal laundry. Children who are old enough to use the equipment should be allowed to do so, with adequate supervision.

8.16 Storage space

Each living unit should contain adequate storage space for household supplies, play materials and craft supplies, holiday decorations, bedding, linen, out-of-season clothing, and luggage, conveniently located and easily accessible to child care staff.

This space should supplement individual closets for children and child care workers and should include storage facilities for personal belongings not currently in use of child care staff.

8.17 Room for child care staff

Each unit should have at least one room with twin beds and private bath reserved for use of staff when on duty and sleeping in. (9.73)

It is preferable for staff to live outside the center, in the community. The salaries of staff members should not be based on the understanding that the agency provides living quarters but should be sufficient for staff members to provide their own.

If on-grounds residence is unavoidable, a private apartment, with living room, bedroom, and bath, should be provided. Rooms for on-duty staff should be located on the same floor as children's bedrooms, so that the child care worker can supervise all children unobtrusively and be available to any of them when needed.

8.18 Residence of executive

The executive should not be required to live in residence. The salary should be set exclusive of residence and should allow the executive to choose where he or she will live.

It is advantageous for the executive and family to live in the community and to take part in community activities. In this way he or she can promote greater understanding of the center and wider interest in it. A staff member on the grounds must be designated to assume responsibility when the executive is at home.

Central Facilities

8.19 Recreation and cultural facilities

In addition to facilities in the individual living units, adequate space and equipment should be available for recreational and cultural programs for all children receiving care. (8.35)

These should include:

- space for active games, dances, dramatics, sports, and any other activity that brings the whole community of children and adults together
- athletic and other recreational equipment
- a room that allows for individual activity such as music practice

The investment in equipment and recreational facilities should be correlated with existing community resources and their accessibility to the children living in the center.

8.20 Outdoor play area

Space allowed for the outside play area should be determined by the number and ages of children in care and the availability of recreational resources in the community.

Space for play should be considered one of the most important parts of the center.

It should be well drained and properly surfaced for all the children to engage in various kinds of activities, with shade and provision for rainy-weather play. There should be space for vegetable and flower gardens, permitting individual garden projects for children, as well as an area for playing ball, building with materials, etc.

Available natural materials, such as sand, water, leaves in the fall, and snow allow for nature play.

8.21 School rooms

An on-grounds school should have classrooms with adequate light and ventilation, and approved equipment and teaching materials.

The school should not be located in a living unit unless adequately separated by means of partitions and its own entrance. (4.16)

The school building should conform to requirements of appropriate education officials and the building codes for the handicapped.

It should be possible to use classrooms after school for children requiring tutoring or remedial teaching. (3.28)

8.22 Chapel

It is preferable to use churches or synagogues in the community rather than a chapel on the grounds. (3.53, 10.4)

Central Services

8.23 Central kitchen

Unit kitchens are preferable. If central food preparation is considered desirable, however, the kitchen should be planned to meet requirements for efficiency, sanitation, and comfortable working conditions. Size and amount of equipment should be determined by the number of persons and the number of meals to be served daily. (8.14)

A well-planned, arranged, and equipped modern kitchen is essential to good food service.

It should be well lighted and equipped for control of heat, odors, and noise. Floors should be greaseproof and easy to clean.

Working areas and location of equipment should be arranged to avoid confusion, waste motion, and cross traffic.

Service units attached to or easily accessible to the kitchen should include: food preparation unit; service space for salads, desserts, beverages, and trays; dairy storage; storage for dry and canned foods and other staples; and a refrigeration unit.

Ample refrigeration should be provided for perishable foods, with separate units for meat, dairy products, and fruits and vegetables, to allow for different temperatures and to prevent tainting of meat and dairy products by other food odors. Deep-freeze units are desirable.

There should be a mechanical sterilizing dishwasher. Municipal, state, or provincial sanitation regulations regarding dishwashing should be met.

Cleaning supplies and equipment should be stored in a different closet from the food.

A high standard of cleanliness and sanitation should be maintained at all times. There should be a separate lavatory for hand washing, in or immediately adjacent to the kitchen.

8.24 Laundry

If a central laundry is operated, it should be conveniently located and have modern equipment and protective devices. (8.15)

Costs of maintaining a laundry or of using a commercial laundry service should be carefully compared, to determine which offers the cheaper and better service.

Room should be allowed for sorting laundry.

8.25 General utility

General utility equipment, including labor-saving devices such as electric cleaners and polishers, should be provided for use of maintenance personnel.

These should be kept in good repair and should be easily accessible in a convenient, well-equipped workroom.

A slop sink and ventilated space for storage of mops should be provided for each level in a building.

Administrative Offices

8.26 Location of offices

Offices of the center should be centrally located and accessible to public transportation. (8.2)

Offices should be soundproofed and insulated from children's living quarters and recreation rooms, and should have a separate entrance.

Parking areas should be provided for families, visitors, and staff.

8.27 Reception areas

The reception room or lobby should convey, by use of color, pictures, children's books and toys, that the center is a place for children, in which they and their families are welcome and understood.

It is important to create the proper atmosphere at the point at which the new child and parents get their first impression of the center.

8.28 Private offices

The executive and other professional staff requiring privacy for interviews, telephoning, and dictating should have separate offices and their own telephones.

If it is necessary to share offices, private rooms should be available for interviewing, telephoning, and dictating.

8.29 Medical facilities

At least one examining and treatment room should be provided for use by physician, dentist, psychiatrist, and psychologist.

It is not desirable for the center to operate its own hospital or infirmary. (3.37, 3.39)

Community resources should be used whenever possible. (3.30)

First aid supplies and prescribed medicines should be stored in a locked cabinet, not accessible to the children.

8.30 Other staff facilities

Administrative offices should provide space for facilities needed by professional staff in performance of their jobs.

These should include:
- rooms for board and staff meetings and group conferences
- staff library
- staff lounge
- rest room facilities for staff and visitors
- rooms for group therapy

8.31 Business and secretarial offices

Offices should be comfortable, attractive, and equipped for efficient operation.

Office space should be partitioned in the interest of efficient work.

Suitable equipment should be maintained in good working condition to permit economical and accurate dictation-transcription, accounting, and statistical reporting.

There should be adequate storage space for office supplies.

A record vault with fire protection, or preferably fire-resistant files that can be locked, will assure protection and preservation of case records.

8.32 Communication system

Interoffice and interbuilding telephones and other communication systems should be installed.

Telephones should be conveniently located and sufficient in number.

Each living unit should have an outside telephone available to both child care staff and children. A non-coin telephone is preferred in the child care office, but a coin telephone may be used by the children.

8.33 Use of commemorative plaques and photographs

Plaques designating gifts, and pictures of benefactors, should not be used in offices, in reception rooms, or over doors of rooms in living units.

Recognition of the contributions of benefactors should be handled with respect and dignity.

Equipment

8.34 Equipment and furnishings

Equipment and furnishings should be easy to clean, attractive, comfortable, durable, adaptable, and designed for efficiency, safety, and the varied everyday use of the children.

> The amount and kind of equipment needed depend on the ages and number of children served. (8.11, 8.12)

> Pictures and other decorative objects should be selected to make art appreciation a part of daily living.

8.35 Leisure and play equipment

All play and leisure equipment should meet standards of the National Recreation Association and should be inspected regularly to avoid safety hazards. (7.10)

> Swimming pools should be enclosed with protective fences and should conform to local health and safety regulations.

8.36 Transportation equipment

The agency should provide adequate and well-insured motor equipment for transport of children and staff.

> A plan for regular inspection and maintenance should ensure safe operation of all vehicles. Both the vehicles and the drivers should meet applicable legal requirements and licensing regulations.

> Safety belts should be installed and used.

> Station wagons and buses should not carry the name of the center, to avoid making children feel different from others and uncomfortable to be so identified.

Sanitation and Safety

Adequate measures should be taken to prevent accidents and to avoid health or safety hazards. The agency should seek approval of the authority having jurisdiction to ensure appropriate protection.

8.37 Requirements for sanitation and safety

Buildings, heating, water supply, sewage disposal, lighting, ventilation, food preparation, fire protection, and other health and safety measures should comply with codes and ordinances established by state, province, county, or city.

Harmful substances and objects, including firearms, that are not essential to agency service should not be kept on the premises. Other poisonous, flammable, and harmful materials should be kept in locked containers, available only to authorized adults. (3.13)

Necessary precautions should be taken to prevent accidents from loose rugs, slippery floors, inadequate lighting, and unsafe play or power equipment; special care should be given to the safety of the handicapped.

Recreational supplies and equipment should also be evaluated for safety. Protected areas should be provided for hazardous activities, e.g., skate boards.

8.38 Heating system

Heating facilities should conform to recommendations of competent mechanical engineers. All heating systems should be installed with safety devices to prevent fires, explosions, and other hazards.

Where heating plants are in the residence unit, they should be enclosed in accordance with building codes and recommended requirements of national standard-setting organizations.

8.39 Fire prevention

All buildings should be located, constructed, and equipped to guard against hazards. All housing for children should comply with state, provincial, and local fire regulations and should be periodically inspected at least once a year.*

All buildings should be carefully examined from the standpoint of

---

* See Life Safety Code, 1976, #101: National Fire Protection Association. See Underwriters' Laboratories of Canada.

maximum fire protection. Fire hazards should be immediately corrected.

All new buildings should be of fire-resistant materials. Old buildings should have sprinkler systems and smoke detectors. An automatic fire control system is important to the safety of children and staff.

Children should not be housed above the first floor without fire escapes approved by the local or state fire marshal. No child should be housed above the second floor.

Smoking areas should be planned when or where appropriate and then approved by the fire marshal.

All electrical and heating installations should be approved by the Underwriters' Laboratory and should be installed accordingly.

Where storage of gasoline, kerosene, fuel oil, or other highly flammable material is necessary, adequate provisions should be made to meet all requirements of safety and fire codes.

8.40 Fire protection

Fire exits, doors, hallways, and stairs should be well lighted and kept clear and ready for use. Fire extinguishers that meet standards of the National Fire Protection Association or the Underwriters' Laboratories of Canada should be installed and inspected regularly and kept charged and filled at all times.

There should be more than one exit from all buildings and from each floor.

All staff should have demonstrations (and some may have training) in the use of extinguishers suitable for different types of fires; this applies especially to child care staff, whose primary responsibility is the children in the living units.

No lock or fastening shall be installed that could inhibit free escape from the inside of any building where children are housed.

8.41 Disaster plans

Effective provisions should be made for the safety of the children and staff in case of fire or other emergency.

The agency should have established plans to deal with disaster and emergencies (such as fires, hurricanes), and all staff should be instructed in the procedures to be followed and their respective duties.

Procedures for evacuation and other emergencies should be posted, reviewed, and tested at frequent and regular intervals to ensure effectiveness and staff readiness.

9

ORGANIZATION AND ADMINISTRATION OF A RESIDENTIAL CENTER

The organization and administration of the agency providing residential services determine the quality of the services offered. Effectiveness of the services for a child and family depends on the caliber, conviction, and understanding of the board of directors; adequacy of financing; availability of necessary resources; knowledge, skill, and personal qualifications of staff; and coordination of all elements of the service.

The Social Agency

9.1 Auspices

Residential services provided as a child welfare service should be administered by a voluntary or public social agency to which responsibility has been delegated by charter or law for children whose parents are unable to provide the care they need.

Agencies may be nonsectarian or under the auspices of church-related, or other religious and fraternal organizations. (10.4)

9.2 Authorization

The agency should be authorized to provide residential services for children by the state department responsible for social services; and should function with a duly constituted charter and bylaws, in accordance with the legal requirements of the state, province, county, or city. The public agency should function in accordance with statutory requirements.

9.3 Incorporation

The voluntary agency should be incorporated under state, provincial, or local requirements. The public agency, as a corporate body, should be properly authorized to administer residential services.

9.4 Licensing

Child welfare residential facilities, under auspices of voluntary and public agencies, should meet licensing requirements. (9.13, 9.15)

Regardless of auspice, minimum licensing requirements and standards should be the same for all agencies.

Board of Directors*

The residential facility should have a board of directors that operates as the governing body of the agency. Although agencies may differ in structure and responsibilities based on statutory requirements, it is important to have active citizen participation in providing residential services for children through a policy-making board or an advisory committee.

9.5 Responsibilities of the board

The board should be responsible for developing policies and program, for evaluating the services given and the continuing need for the service in relation to changing conditions and other resources in the community.

The board should delegate full administrative responsibility to the executive director and take no direct responsibility for administering the program or working with individual children.

---

* Guide for Board Organization in Social Agencies, New York; Child Welfare League of America, 1975, pp. 7, 3.

Specific board responsibilities are:
- to determine the purpose and function of the agency (1.1, 9.14)
- to formulate policies and a program that can best meet the needs of the children and parents for whom it has undertaken to provide service (9.15)
- to ensure availability of the funds, resources, and equipment required to carry out the agency's purpose and to interpret financial needs (9.11, 9.12)
- to supervise expenditure of funds (9.10)
- to determine personnel policies (9.71)
- to select a qualified executive (9.36)
- to evaluate regularly the kind and quality of service children are receiving and the need for any change (9.78)
- to set up procedures that will provide channels of communication between the board and executive and between board and staff (9.19)
- to bring to the agency the concerns and unmet needs of the community
- to engage in action on broad social issues and problems affecting child welfare (9.9–9.13)
- to keep informed about the philosophy and standards of public and voluntary child welfare services, including services for children and families in their own homes, or in other ways such as guardianship, foster family, adoption, etc.
- to represent the agency in the community and to interpret its program with the help of the executive and other staff members (9.81, 9.82)

9.6 Board composition

The board or advisory committee should consist of a sufficient number of members, both men and women, to be representative of the various religious, business, professional, cultural, and ethnic groups in the community and in groups served by the agency.

Board members should be selected who have genuine concern about children. They should have the personal qualifications, interests, time, and ability to become informed about their board responsibilities and to participate fully and consistently in carrying them out.

In voluntary and public agencies, no member of the board should be a paid trustee, active client, employee, or agent, or receive a fee for services rendered to the agency. The business or professional firm of the board member should not be included in any financial transaction of the agency.

9.7 Change of board composition

A plan for periodic change of board composition should assure an active, enlightened, and effective board that provides for continuity of leadership, long-range goals, and changing points of view.

9.8 Board committees

Standing or special committees of the board should be established by the board.

Actively functioning committees for board operation include executive, nominating, finance or budget, program or children's services, personnel, public relations, public policy, and grounds committees.

Additional standing or ad hoc committees, composed of board and staff members as appropriate, may be necessary to carry out effectively the work of the board.

The function and authority of each committee should be defined specifically. The committee should fulfill a definite need, and have a clearly stated charge and a specified time for reporting back to the board.

Participation of staff members or committees with selected board committees, e.g., personnel, promotes better understanding of agency program and appreciation of the respective responsibilities of board and staff. The board thus has a formal means of appropriate staff participation in its determination of policy. (9.36)

9.9 Advisory committees

In the public agency there should be an advisory committee for each residential service under its auspices, or an advisory committee to the agency or department that carries responsibility for residential services.

Advisory committees provide for citizen participation and exchange of points of view.

The advisory committee should be responsible for keeping well informed about the particular service, for helping the administrative authority to be informed about it, and for making recommendations when changes or new policies are needed.

Minutes should be kept as a record of committee decisions.

Financing and Costs

9.10 Budget

The agency should have financial resources and a budget that permit it to carry out its responsibilities in accordance with approved standards of practice.

The budget should provide for meeting direct costs of care for the children the agency undertakes to serve, with allowance for their special needs, for adequate salaries and opportunities for continued staff development, for a sufficient number of qualified staff, and for adequate maintenance of physical facilities.

The number of children served and the scope of the agency's services should be no greater than will permit an acceptable standard of service to be maintained with the available funds.

An annual functional budget should be compiled in advance, with estimates of each unit of agency operation separately computed. It should be reviewed throughout the year.

The board should authorize the executive to make expenditures within the total budget as approved for the year. Any substantial variations in income or expenditure from the prepared estimates, and proposals to transfer funds from one classification to another, should be referred to the board for consideration and action.

9.11 Costs of service

Costs should be computed in a way that reflects the component parts and quality of the service offered, the purpose of the agency, and the needs and problems of the children served.

Costs will depend on:
- characteristics of children for whom service is given, such as age and nature of problems (1.5)
- qualifications and number of staff members providing services (9.32–9.66)
- scope of program (1.7)
- physical plant and requirements of operating and maintaining it (8.1–8.39)

Generally accepted procedures should determine direct and indirect costs and allowable and nonallowable expenditures.

Costs should include administrative costs as well as costs of care and direct services to children and parents.

9.12 Sources of support

Residential facilities may be financed from voluntary contributions from individuals, groups, and organizations; public tax funds; income from endowments; and payments from parents.

Sources of voluntary agency financing should include voluntary contributions. The agency should expect parents to meet all or part of the cost of the child's care, according to their ability to do so, through direct payments and through funds to which the child is entitled, such as Social Security, military service benefits, and other insurances. (2.19)

Fees for purchase of care by a public agency and fees charged to parents should be based on full cost of the service on the basis not only of actual costs of the previous year but on estimated current per capita costs of service rendered, reflecting changing costs.

9.13 Audit

Every agency should have an independent annual audit of income and expenditures by a certified public accountant employed and paid by the agency.

The agency should show evidence of sound financial operation.

Policies and practices governing receipt and expenditure of money should be in accordance with sound budgeting, disbursement, and audit control procedures.

There should be full disclosure of financial transactions with the agency, e.g., ownership and leases, that involve board and staff members and their immediate families.

Policies and Procedures

9.14 Function and purpose

The agency should clearly define and periodically evaluate its responsibility, the services it is prepared to offer, the children it accepts for care and treatment, and the geographical area covered.

The functions and services of the agency should be related to the child care needs of the community and to other available community services.

The agency should evaluate its services systematically to determine whether it is meeting the needs of the children accepted for care and whether it is meeting a child welfare need in the community.

It should be ready to adapt its services to changing needs as they reflect changing social, economic, and cultural conditions, and the growth of knowledge of sound care and treatment of children.

It is generally preferable for child welfare agencies to provide multiple services, including foster care, adoption, and residential care, as well as services for the child who lives at home, so that appropriate services can be expeditiously selected for the child as they are needed.

9.15 Policies and procedures

The agency should operate on the basis of written policies and procedures subscribed to and reviewed periodically by the board of directors and administered by the executive. (9.5, 9.36)

Written statements of purposes and objectives, services offered, eligibility requirements for service (intake policies), and policies and procedures in implementing services should be available to board, staff, and other interested persons. (9.16)

9.16 Agency manual

A manual should be compiled for use by board and staff, reviewed annually, and revised periodically to keep it up-to-date with current agency and professional practices.

The manual should include the history, charter, and bylaws of the agency.

It should also incorporate the statement defining functions, purposes, services, policies, and procedures. (9.15)

9.17 Departmentalization and decentralization

When needed for efficiency or necessity, the agency should departmentalize or decentralize certain parts of its service. (9.40, 9.41)

In large multiservice agencies, components of the service may need to be centralized, e.g., intake, group living. However, decentralization may be necessary when an agency serves a broad geographic area so that it will be better able to provide service.

9.18 Coordination and integration

It is essential to make administrative provision for coordination of the various parts of the service, and for planning and integration of the total service given in behalf of each child. (1.9, 1.10, 9.19)

It is the administration's responsibility to create an atmosphere of respect and trust among all staff members and with cooperating programs or agencies.

All components of the service should be related to one another and should be directed to a common goal.

The value and treatment aspects of each part must be understood by all staff members. Their roles and responsibilities must be clearly defined and their contributions recognized and respected.

Formalization of agency relationships among different services and programs within the agency or among community agencies can lead to coordination of multiple services for the child and family. A wider range of services can thus be available for the children and families to enable an individualized and well-focused service to be given. (10.5)

9.19 Communication

Definite channels of communication should be established and used regularly to ensure coordination of agency functions and integration of services.

These should include:
- regularly scheduled case conferences attended by all staff members involved in the service for a particular child
- general staff meetings
- departmental staff meetings
- regularly scheduled conferences of staff members with their supervisors (8.68)
- regularly planned conferences of the administrator with department heads

These meetings should serve to orient staff at every level to the philosophy and objectives of the agency and assure that roles and responsibilities of each staff member are understood and respected by others.

Open channels of communication to the executive are particularly important to ensure accessibility to suggestions from any staff member, so that the executive is kept informed about what is going on as it affects the services for the children and the policies of the agency.

9.20 Procedures for appeal

The agency should provide a workable procedure that can be readily used in behalf of a child when the care, services, or plans for the child are considered unsatisfactory by the parents or guardian.

All procedures for appeal should be made known to the parents or other legal guardian, to all staff members, and to older children in placement.

If a voluntary agency is providing service through connection with a public agency, provision should be made for complaints to be lodged with the administrative staff of the agency providing service, and where indicated or preferred, with the public agency that is responsible for the child.

Legal Responsibility of the Agency

9.21 Assumption of responsibility for children

The agency providing residential service should be empowered, by voluntary agreement with the parents or legal custodians, or through judicial action, to assume responsibility for the custody of each child accepted for care.

The public agency as well as the voluntary agency should be able to accept children for foster care directly from their parents or guardians, without court action.

Routine or arbitrary abridgment of parental rights should not be a requirement for a child receiving service from the agency. (2.17)

Unnecessary limitation of parental rights may weaken family ties and feelings of mutual responsibility, and prolong placement far beyond a time consistent with the child's well-being.

Parents who need and want residential care for a child should not be compelled to go through the court or be deprived of legal custody of their child simply for the purpose of obtaining public funds for support of the child or for the convenience of the agency.

The agency should have in its files a written agreement from the parents, or valid documentation from a proper court, that establishes the child's custody and authorizes placement in the residential facility. (9.25)

9.22 Legal custody

If temporary abridgment of parental rights is necessary for the welfare of the child, the agency should assume only those rights that are essential for its service to the child, and should operate consistently within the framework of the rights it has assumed and the rights that the child's parents retain. (2.17)

An agency may have custody of a child by virtue of an agreement with a parent, but it does not have legal custody unless such custody is bestowed by a court. It is the legal custody or guardianship of the child that is transferred by the court to an agency in cases in which a child is found to be neglected, abused, or delinquent, and the court determines that the child must live away from his or her own home.

In judicial proceedings regarding custody of the child, legal representation for the child should be assured.

It should be recognized that when the court awards legal custody of a child to the agency providing residential service, the parents' exercise of their rights and responsibilities is temporarily limited but not terminated.

9.23 Guardianship of the person

The agency should make certain that each child has a legally responsible individual who exercises rights of guardianship of the person. The agency should be prepared to bring to the attention of the legal custodian or the court the need for appropriate court proceedings on behalf of any child for whom determination of guardianship becomes necessary.

Every child is entitled to a guardian of the person, either a natural guardian by birth, or by adoption, or by judicial appointment of a guardian who will safeguard the interests and make the important decisions in the life of the child while maintaining a personal relationship with him or her.

When a child has no parents, or where parental rights have been terminated, it is preferable to select as a guardian for the child an interested relative or family friend otherwise qualified, if such a person is available, to help maintain family and community ties. Appointment of persons employed by or associated with agencies holding physical or legal custody may not only limit personal ties, but also may involve a conflict between official duties and loyalties as a member of the agency and as a guardian of the child.

When, however, a child is awaiting placement for adoption, the agency that holds legal custody or plans to place him for adoption may be appointed for a limited period of time as guardian of the person or the child, until adoption has been consummated or guardianship is terminated by a court order.

Circumstances under which it may be necessary to transfer guardianship of the person from the parents and vest it in another person would include death or unavailability of the parents, abandonment, improper care or protection, and termination of parental rights when the child has been relinquished for adoption and an adoptive home is yet to be found.

9.24 Termination of parental rights

The placement agency or the agency holding legal custody should be prepared to request the court to terminate parental rights and responsibilities when it has been established that the parents will be unable or unwilling in the foreseeable future to fulfill their responsibilities in giving care, love, and protection to the child. (2.18, 6.13)

To ensure adequate protection for the parents and to effect binding, clearly understood legal results, any action to limit or terminate parental rights must be taken by proper legal procedure in a court of competent jurisdiction.

Termination should be considered so that new and permanent ties for the child can be created through adoption in situations in which:

- children have been left in foster care for extended periods, with parents showing lack of continuing interest or ability to give proper parental care and protection
- abandonment has taken place
- parents have voluntarily relinquished parental rights (except when, by statutory procedures, relinquishment is deemed to terminate parental rights)

9.25 Legal status of child

In accepting a child for residential care, the agency should be responsible for determining who has legal custody or guardianship, especially in instances of separation or divorce, court commitment, or birth out of wedlock. When necessary, the agency should have access to legal counsel to clarify the status of children under care.

> Planning for each child should explicitly take into account his or her legal relationship to parents, family members, and agencies providing care for the child.

9.26 Periodic review of children under care

The agency should review, at least annually, all children under care to determine in each case the plan for termination of its service. (1.1, 2.14, 2.23, 9.24)

> To ensure planning for the stability of a child, the agency should cooperate with foster care review boards established by statute, the judiciary, or the state administration.

Statistics, Reporting, and Records

9.27 Statistics on children in care

The agency should maintain and report accurate statistics, as follows, on the children who use its services, in cooperation with community, state, and national reporting systems:

- a permanent file, with a separate sheet for each child admitted, giving name, sex, race, religion, birthdate, birthplace; names of parents, brothers, and sisters; names of persons with whom the child was living at the time of admission; date of admission; date of discharge; name and address of person to whom discharged; legal guardian
- an annual census of children under care
- a monthly statistical report of applications, admissions, discharge, and other data requested by the state or public department and the provincial authorities responsible for child welfare; community planning and funding bodies; and other organizations where indicated
- computerization is increasingly relied upon for quick and accurate tracking

9.28 Administrative information

The agency should have a ready means, such as computerization, of collecting, maintaining, and supplying administrative information needed for both its own accountability and an understanding of its services.

The agency should have a means of collecting information:

- to identify problem areas or situations requiring administrative or staff attention, e.g., critical events, medication usage, etc.
- to assist evaluation of the agency's operation and performance
- for timeliness of agency reports required on behalf of a child or on aspects of the agency's programs
- to prepare for the agency's accounting functions

Participation in community-wide reporting of appropriate administrative data to councils of social agencies, state, federal, and provincial departments responsible for child welfare programs, and on request to other organizations such as the Child Welfare League of America, makes possible broader data collection for planning child welfare services for the kinds and numbers of children needing residential services, for research to improve services, and for financial resources needed to support the programs for children in residential care. Such participation should follow assurance of preservation of confidentiality.

9.29 Purpose of case records

The agency should maintain an up-to-date record of each child and family to indicate, from the point of intake until termination of services, the responsibility assumed for each child, how the responsibility is carried out, and the effectiveness of the service.

The case record may be used for:

- planning for each child and assuring continuity of service despite staff changes
- understanding and evaluating problems of the child and family and their capacity for dealing with them
- evaluating quality and quantity of service
- supervising workers
- teaching staff and students
- accountability to the community

9.30 Form and content of case records

Although the form and content of case records may vary from agency to agency in relation to the purpose of the individual record, all records should include the information needed for providing service for the child and family, for planning, and for periodic reevaluation, as well as essential information that should be retained for use at some future time for or by the child.

The agency should determine the purpose that its case records should serve.

The purpose of the case record should be the basis for selecting the method of recording and the content of the record.

Case records should not become a miscellaneous collection of items of information that are saved because they might someday be found useful.

Necessary information includes:

- factual data and identifying information: name, date, and place of birth; sex; religion; race; names and addresses of parents, brothers and sisters, close relatives; guardianship and custody; date of admission
- verification of birth and legal status
- statement signed by parents, relatives, or guardians consenting to placement and including agreement with parents regarding such items as continuing financial responsibility and amounts to be paid; or statement from a proper court or agency vesting legal custody in the agency; and authorization for medical and surgical treatment
- intake study, including referral material from other agencies or court, and reason for decision to accept child for residential care
- diagnostic summary and evaluation at time of admission, including statement of problem necessitating use of residential care
- treatment plan and goals at time of admission, including determination of who will carry responsibility for work with child and family
- periodic summaries of child's development, functioning, progress, and response to services given, including child care, social work, recreation, and psychotherapy
- periodic summaries of services to parents and contracts with them
- reports of significant incidents, both positive and negative (e.g., school achievement, running away), and changes in family situation (e.g., marital status, birth of other children)
- health record: summary of health history, illnesses, treatment received; reports of medical examinations; consent of parents for medical and surgical treatment and hospitalization
- school reports, including teachers' evaluations of progress

- reports of psychological and psychiatric examinations
- summaries of quarterly staff evaluation conferences, including social work, child care, medical, psychiatric, psychological, and school staff members
- periodic evaluations and modifications of plan or treatment goals
- closing summary (at time of departure from the center)
- plan for aftercare
- date of final discharge; name, address, and relationship of person(s) or organization to whom discharged; guardianship status

9.31 Confidentiality

Each member of staff and every volunteer should be required to respect the privacy of the children and their families and to act accordingly. (6.17, 9.80)

The agency's written policies should cover the many facets of confidentiality, including legislative and administrative regulations.

Staff members, volunteers, and bodies of governance should be fully informed of current agency policy and regulations protecting the privacy of the children and their families.

It is necessary that the children and their families know about the policies and also about legislation, regulations, and funding bodies that require disclosure of personal information. Ordinarily, any decision to release personal information requires the consent of the parent and/or the older child. Exceptions to this principle should be discussed with them so that they understand the conditions for using the service.

Many issues concerning agency responsibility for confidentiality are under community, governmental, and judicial review. As one aspect of its disclosure policy, the agency should evaluate any request for personal information, the likelihood of maintenance of confidentiality by a third party, and the pertinence of the requested information.

The identity of a child used in any publicity should be given only if a positive value accrues to the child; the written consent of a parent or guardian should be obtained before using a child or picture of a child in any publicity.

Staffing

Not all residential services will need all categories of staff. The responsibilities listed for the various position should, however, be assigned among the members of staff who are qualified to carry them.

The quality of the services for children and their families depends largely on the personal qualifications, knowledge, and skill of staff members.

9.32 Size of staff

A sufficient number of qualified staff members should be available to perform effectively the tasks required in providing the total service for the children accepted for care and for their parents and families. (2.1–2.26)

The number of staff members and the positions required should be determined by the size and purposes of the residential care program.

9.33 Workloads

The number of children assigned to individual staff members should be limited to the extent necessary for fulfillment of the agency's responsibility to provide effective service for each child and family.

Certain variables should be taken into account in determining the size of an individual workload of a child care worker, a social worker, or teacher, such as the:

- nature of problems and other characteristics of children accepted for care (1.5)
- number of cases in which intensive work with the children or with parents is required (3.3, 9.55)
- amount of time required for individual and staff conferences and recording
- amount of time required for consultation and preparation for it
- responsibilities other than direct work with child or parents, such as committee or community activities

9.34 Job definition

Responsibilities of each member of the staff or a particular job classification should be administratively defined in writing so that each staff member may understand his or her responsibilities and work effectively in carrying them out.

Minimum education and experience requirements for each position should be specified in each written job description. In small centers, and at times in any center, one staff member may carry several responsibilities. These should be responsibilities that do not conflict with one another.

9.35 Personal characteristics of the staff

Each staff member should be selected on the basis of personal characteristics that have been found desirable in working with children in groups, and in residential care, in addition to the requirements of education, experience, and competence for the particular job.

These characteristics should apply to all staff members in all categories and also to volunteers. (9.36–9.66)

It should be recognized that working in residential care makes special demands on staff, because of the:

- emotional strain of working with a large number of children and adults who present a variety of problems
- necessity of recognizing and respecting the contribution of each staff member and relating his or her role to that of other staff members
- importance of serving as part of a team that works within the objectives, policies, and procedures of the agency

All staff members should be responsive to children and feel comfortable with them.

All staff members should be in good health and have the energy and capacity to handle the physical work and the pressures of active children. Flexibility and the capacity and desire to learn are essential. (9.75)

Men and women should be employed and they should include members of the racial, ethnic, and cultural groups of the children served, at various staff levels. (9.45, 9.76)

All staff members should be able to work with others and be willing to share responsibility.

Administrative Staff

9.36 Responsibilities of the executive

The executive director should be delegated by the board to carry overall responsibility for all children in care; to administer the services of the agency; to plan and coordinate all phases of the program and services within the framework of functions and policies established by the board; to evaluate continually the effectiveness of services for children and parents; and to seek new approaches and knowledge.

The executive's responsibilities include:

- directing the agency program
- representing the agency in the community
- delegating appropriate responsibilities to staff (9.34)
- recruiting, employing, supervising, training, and discharging staff (9.35, 9.71, 9.76)
- providing leadership for all departments
- providing professional help to the board in carrying out its responsibilities, interpreting to board members the needs of the children, making recommendations when a change of policy seems desirable, and assisting them in periodic evaluation of the agency's services (9.5, 9.14, 9.15)
- preparing the annual budget for board consideration, keeping the board informed of financial needs, and operating within the established budget (9.10)
- supervising building maintenance, management, and purchasing
- participating with the board in interpreting the need for financial support of the agency, even when the agency is supported through federated fund raising (9.11, 9.12)

The executive should attend all board and committee meetings. (9.8)

9.37 Qualifications of the executive

The executive should have:

- respect and concern for the welfare of children
- professional education at the master's degree level in an appropriate discipline, i.e., social work, child care, specialized education
- training or experience in the principles and functions of organizational administration
- a minimum of four years of increasingly responsible supervisory and administrative experience in a social agency or other service setting that serves children, adolescents, or both, with at least one year in a residential setting

    The executive is the key person in the residential service and determines the quality of the service as he or she carries out responsibility for selection and supervision of staff, for administrative procedures, for coordination, and for leadership.

The executive must have characteristics and demonstrated skills essential for the administration of a residential center:

- physical health, ability to work hard, and to withstand stresses and strains of administering a complex program
- understanding of administrative theory and practice
- ability to deal with staff, to select qualified staff, to delegate responsibility so that staff members can work independently, to give staff support and recognition, to create a team spirit, and to command respect and confidence
- ability to organize and coordinate
- understanding of group living: how children's needs can be met through the group, the possibilities and limitations of environmental treatment in relation to the total service
- understanding of and skill in both individual and group approaches
- knowledge of residential management, purchasing, building maintenance

9.38 Assistant to the executive

Because of the 24-hour responsibility in residential care, it is necessary to have one or more assistants to whom administrative responsibilities can be delegated.

In general, qualifications should be the same as those of the executive, but with less experience when employed.

An assistant to the executive may also carry responsibility for direction of the treatment service (9.39), or supervision of the group living program.

9.39 Responsibility for program coordination

The program coordinator should be responsible to the executive for planning, executing, and supervising the program of service and care. Qualifications include education and experience at the master's degree level or above in an appropriate discipline.

Responsibilities include:

- coordination of social work, education, recreation, health services, and daily living programs
- determining that the plan for each child is carried out in the daily living program

- coordination of the activities of dietitian, cook, and maintenance supervisor with the rest of the program

Experience in staff supervision and training is necessary for understanding the problems and special needs of all staff members.

The program coordinator must have knowledge about the interrelationships between child development, family interaction, personality disorders, group behavior, child care, and social work.

9.40 Supervisory staff

Regardless of the size of the residential facility, lines of authority should be clearly designated so that there is a supervisor to whom each worker is administratively and professionally responsible. (9.17, 9.68)

Supervisory staff includes those responsible for supervision of group living, social work, business management, and maintenance. (9.41, 9.51, 9.52, 9.68)

Supervisory staff should have professional training and experience in their own specialization.

In the small residential facility with only one social worker, psychologist, or teacher, continuing professional development through appropriate supervision or consultation must be provided.

9.41 Supervisor of child care staff

The supervisor of child care staff should be responsible to the program coordinator; minimum qualifications include a master's degree in social work or other human service and four years of experience in child care.

Responsibilities of the child care supervisor include recruitment, training, and supervision of child care staff. (9.42, 9.68, 9.69, 9.76)

Child Care Staff

Child care staff members should have at least a high school education as a background for learning what is needed to perform their role in the care of children. (9.44)

9.42 Selection of child care staff

Child care workers should be selected after assessing their capacity to understand children with special needs and their ability and willingness to further their knowledge and skills in working with the kinds of children for whom the service is provided.

The process should include personal interviews and references.

A new staff member should be assigned to work for a period of time with an experienced child care staff member who can observe reactions and questions and can help in assessing potential for work with children.

Before being given primary responsibility for a group of children, an untrained or new child care worker should have training in child care, should serve an apprenticeship with one or more experienced child care workers, and receive a positive job performance evaluation.

9.43 Personal qualities of child care staff

Child care staff members should be selected on the basis of personal characteristics that qualify them to work with children.

Child care workers should be:

- comfortable for children to be with
- able to respect and understand children, to get along with them, and to be responsive to their needs and feelings
- capable of earning the respect of children and of representing qualities and values with which children can identify
- able to assume authority and to control a group without having to be bossy, punitive, threatening, or competitive with children on their level
- able to assume different roles for different children
- able to develop and maintain group spirit
- capable of initiating, participating in, and enjoying some children's activities
- capable of tolerating deviant behavior and of dealing with aggressive behavior and hostility and recognizing that it is not necessarily directed at them
- able to maintain firm, consistent, and objective attitudes
- strong enough to withstand the physical and emotional strains of caring for active and often disturbed children and to rebound after periods of tension
- involved in continuing activities and interests outside of the facility and not entirely dependent upon the children for personal satisfaction

- able to work together with many other persons in all the staff categories
- able to accept supervision and to learn new ways of dealing with situations

9.44 Educational requirements for child care staff

Child care workers should have at least a high school diploma, or its equivalent, or meet the requirements of certification; it is desirable for child care workers to have some specialized training in such areas as child development or mental health. (9.41)

> The agency should provide inservice training and supervision to enhance understanding of child care practice. (5.6)

> Promising young workers should be encouraged to obtain professional education and the agency should provide leaves of absence for this purpose.

9.45 Sex of child care staff

Child care staff members of both sexes should be employed so that children may have the opportunity for relationships with both men and women. ,

> It is important for boys and girls to have someone of the same sex with whom they can identify and someone of the opposite sex to whom they can learn to relate successfully.

> Men and women should be selected on the basis of their individual qualifications rather than because they are married to one another.

> If couples are employed, each should be capable of carrying specific responsibilities in relation to the children.

Other Group-Living Staff Members

9.46 Recreation staff

Staff members who carry out the recreation program should be selected on the basis of experience with groups of children whose recreational needs and interests vary. They should be able to work with the supervisor of the group living program to create a rich program of child-centered, rather than program-centered, activities correlated with group living.

A recreation program requires enough staff to plan, coordinate, and supervise this activity. Staff members should have a variety of skills in organized group activities, such as athletics, arts and crafts, woodworking, dramatics, and art.

They should have experience in play activities that can engage the shifting interests and short attention spans of individual children or the group.

They should be energetic and resourceful and able to enjoy children through play.

At the same time, they should be able to recognize that not all children can enter into competitive activities and that some children may not want to for a particular time.

Recreation workers should be familiar with community resouces, for supplementing their activities on the grounds and offering a more diversified program.

Specialized workers should have a bachelor's or master's degree in recreation.

9.47 Nutritionist

The services of a professional nutritionist should be available for consultation on planning and providing nutrition and food service (purchase and preparation) and for supervision of staff members who prepare food for the children. (3.16)

The nutritionist should meet the requirements of certification by the American Dietetic Association and be experienced in nutrition services for groups of children.

The size of the agency will determine whether a nutritionist should be employed as a full-time member of the staff.

The nutritionist should have knowledge not only of the nutritional requirements of children but of their emotional needs in relation to food, and should be able to adapt menus, with particular attention to children whose previous diets have been inadequate, who need special diets, or whose food preferences have been influenced by cultural and family backgrounds that differ from the majority of the population.

9.48 Housekeeping and maintenance staff

The number of staff members employed should be sufficient to carry on the everyday housekeeping and maintenance of buildings and grounds. (5.9)

The need for different kinds of personnel for these functions depends on the size and type of center.

The manager of maintenance should have sufficient staff to carry out all the duties of cleaning and laundry; other duties include but are not limited to those of porter, janitor, chauffeur, mechanic, and gardener.

Employment of one or more full-time cooks will depend on the number of children to be fed and the pattern of food preparation. Where food is prepared in the individual living units, child care workers should not be routinely used as cooks. (5.9)

Housekeeping and maintenance staff should be selected not only on the basis of ability to perform their job assignments, but with due consideration of their attitudes toward children and their personal qualities. They should be able to accept the philosophy and program of the center. (9.35)

Opportunities for inservice training and channels of communication should be provided so that they can understand the program and carry out their work in consonance with it.

Office Management

9.49 Office staff

A sufficient number of managerial and support staff members should be employed to carry out the business, secretarial, and clerical duties, such as maintenance of records, correspondence, fiscal matters and bookkeeping, so that the services of the agency can be carried out.

The staff should be oriented to the goals of the agency program and to the confidential nature of the job, and should be able to relate to the special needs of children in care. (9.31)

Staff members should be qualified for their respective responsibilities.

Social Work Staff

The majority of social workers should have a master's degree in social work.

9.50 Social work director

Depending on the size of the agency, responsibility for administering the social work program and for providing leadership and continual improvement of the quality of social work practice should be carried by the director of social work or by a social work supervisor designated to assume this responsibility by the coordinator of treatment services.

In addition to graduate education, the social work director should have had at least five years of experience as a social work supervisor, including supervision of direct social work with children with personality problems, preferably children who have lived in a residential facility or other group setting.

9.51 Social work supervisor

There should be one social work supervisor for not more than five social workers, carrying responsibility for professional development, inservice training, and supervision.

A minimum of four years of experience in social work practice, individual and group, should be required and should include some experience in an agency providing services to children.

In a small agency, the responsibilities of the social work director and supervisor may be carried by one staff member. In larger agencies, the supervisor is responsible to the social work director.

9.52 Graduate social workers

Graduate social workers should carry responsibility for casework and groupwork with individual children and their parents.

In addition to a master's in social work, social workers should have experience or field work in an agency providing child welfare services, skill in working with children in placement and their parents, and (for at least one or more on the staff) skill in casework and groupwork with children with emotional and behavioral problems.

It is important to have both men and women as social workers in a residential center.

Special requirements for social workers include:
• ability to communicate with children and parents

- conviction about the child's need to belong to his or her own family and about the rights of children and parents
- skills developed in placement and direct treatment of children and families and the meaning and effects of separation from and return to the family
- understanding of a total service for a child and family, including environmental treatment
- understanding of children and families of various cultural and racial groups
- ability to work as a member of a team and to use the contributions of other staff members
- knowledge of community resources and legislation pertaining to child welfare

When outside social work therapists are employed for particular children, they should meet the agency's educational and experience requirements and those of the standard-setting organization for clinical practice. (3.46, 9.57)

9.53 Social groupworker

Social workers who carry responsibility for groupwork services should have a master's degree in social work with specialization in social groupwork; experience in the field of groupwork with children; and, if responsible for supervision of child care staff, experience in a child care residential facility.

Responsibilities of the groupworker will depend on the size of the center and the design of its program.

If it is necessary to employ social workers without experience in groupwork methods, provision should be made for additional training and consultation by a social groupworker.

9.54 Social workers

The agency that employs social workers without a master's degree in social work should provide supervision by social workers with a master's degree as well as inservice training, and should define clearly the duties and responsibilities of the nongraduate workers to ensure that their assignments are commensurate with their level of competence, skill, and development.

The majority of social workers should have a master's degree in social work; however, staff members with less education may carry out some social work responsibilities.

Such staff members should have the educational qualifications for admission to and interest in acquiring, graduate education. Leaves of absence to complete training within a specified time limit should be offered.

9.55 Workload of social workers

Size of workloads of social workers should be determined by the different units of service required for each assigned case (e.g., intake, social work, treatment of children and their parents, aftercare), frequency of the different units of service, changes in frequency of the different units of service, and time needed for each unit.

It has been estimated that the maximum number of children, including their parents, that can be served by a full-time social worker in a residential facility is 12–15. To maintain effectiveness and limit worker turnover, it is important to avoid overloading a worker. Inability to provide adequate service to all clients is a prime source of frustration and burnout.

When an agency uses workload management techniques, supervisors can balance caseloads and guard against overloading their workers. With appropriate workloads, social workers should be able to plan, select, and deliver appropriate services, resulting in improved service delivery.

Specialists and Consultants

Specialists as members of the staff should, in addition to performing their own functions, offer consultation to other staff members regarding problems relevant to the consultant's special knowledge and training.

9.56 Basis for employment

Specialists and consultants should be employed full-time or part-time as regular members of the staff on a salary or fee basis. Their roles should be clearly defined.

9.57 Qualifications for all consultants and specialists

All specialists should meet the requirements for training and for membership in the standard-setting organization in their particular professional fields. In addition, they should have personal characteristics that make it possible for them to work with children with special needs and to collaborate with other staff members. (9.35, 9.58–9.65)

They should be willing and able to identify with the philosophy and goals of the agency and to provide services in such a manner that they form an integral part of the total service of the agency.

9.58 Medical staff

The agency should employ at least one pediatrician, or, as appropriate, a specialist in adolescence, on a salary or fee basis as a full-time or part-time member of the staff, to act as consultant to the agency in formulating and carrying out its policies for health and medical care. He or she should be administratively responsible to the executive for planning and supervising the health services and coordinating them with the total program. (3.29–3.43)

Any physician providing services on a salary or fee basis should be regarded as a member of the staff responsible to the physician directing the health program.

Services of medical specialists, such as a gynecologist or neurologist, should be available when needed for any child. Salaries or fees should accord with prevailing rates in the community.

9.59 Dentist

A dentist with experience in dental work with children should be responsible for the direction of the dental program. (3.43)

9.60 Nurse

Depending on the number of children in care, a nurse, preferably with experience as well as training in public health service, may be on call or on staff, as a full-time or part-time staff member, or through arrangements for nursing service such as Visiting Nurses Association or other community resource. (3.42)

The services of a nurse should be available at all times.

The nurse should be responsible to a physician for all medical aspects of the work.

Regular administrative consultation with a staff member who can interpret the needs of individual children is desirable.

9.61 Psychiatric consultant

Services of a psychiatrist experienced in treatment of children should be available to the agency on a retainer basis for a stipulated number of hours per week, depending on the number of children served, the nature of their problems, and the availability of community mental health services. (3.44)

The psychiatrist should be fully qualified, with special training in the psychology of children.

The psychiatrist must be able to give consultation and recommendations about treatment in a way that enables staff members to make the fullest use of their own skills.

The psychiatrist should have time to attend all major staff meetings, case conferences, and other meetings that serve to integrate the treatment of individual children with the agency program.

9.62 Psychologist

Services of a clinical psychologist should be available through employment as a full- or part-time staff member or through arrangements with another agency in the community. (3.45)

The psychologist should be fully qualified (generally with a doctorate in clinical psychology) and have had experience working with children.

9.63 Teaching staff

When there is a school in the residential facility, the principal and teachers should be fully qualified by specialized training and experience to conduct the school program in accordance with the best current practices in special education. (4.14)

Teachers may also be employed as members of the staff to help children who require individual tutoring or remedial education. (3.28)

All teachers should have special education and skills for working with children with emotional and social problems and learning difficulties, and should be currently certified by educational officials.

9.64 Other specialists

The agency should have access to community resources or should employ specialists on a regular basis for treatment of the special needs of individual children. (9.57)

9.65 Religious consultant

A religious consultant, such as a pastor or rabbi, should be employed on a full-time or part-time basis as a member of the staff when the special needs of a group of children require on-grounds religious services. (3.52)

It is preferable to have a religious consultant with clinical training in a social agency or mental hospital during theological training or after the assumption of pastoral duties. Thus, the consultant will have an orientation to child welfare and familiarity with treatment of social and emotional problems, and be able, as needed, to serve as a member of the professional team helping the child and family with their problems.

Whenever possible, religious participation and training should be made available to the children through use of community resources.

Volunteers

9.66 Selection and training of volunteers

The agency should establish requirements for selection of volunteers and should provide orientation and supervision. (3.55)

The volunteer's responsibility should be clearly differentiated from that of recreation, child care, and other staff members and should not take the place of requisite paid personnel.

A training program should be planned to orient volunteers to the purpose, goals, and philosophy of the agency and to increase their skills as they gain experience.

The agency that uses volunteers must have appropriate staff who can be assigned to select, evaluate, and supervise them and must provide appropriate recognition of the volunteers' contribution to the program.

Volunteers should be assigned only to those activities that accord with their skills and qualifications.

It is important to keep turnover of volunteers to a minimum. Training and recognition help an agency to· keep its volunteers.

Staff Development

9.67 Staff development program

To maintain standards of service, a continuing development program should be carried on.

Each staff member should have the help needed to make the fullest use of knowledge and skill that he or she already has and to develop special skills needed in working with children in group care.

In addition, each staff member should have the opportunity to increase his or her competence by keeping abreast of current developments or by assimilating and evaluating new ideas and techniques, particularly those relating to specific duties.

A comprehensive staff development program should provide:
* supervision and inservice training
* educational or sabbatical leave, with scholarship or stipend for qualified staff members to obtain further training
* time off for attendance at professional meetings, conferences, and workshops, with budgetary provision for meeting the expenses involved
* psychiatric seminars
* a professional library accessible to all staff with basic books and publications for child care staff in a central library and in the living units

9.68 Supervision

Regular supervision should be available as appropriate to every staff member, in accordance with that person's training, experience, and maturity. (9.40)

Supervision includes individual and group supervision, with consultation increasing as members achieve sufficient experience.

The use, method, and amount of supervision may vary, but should carry out the three-fold purpose of supervision:

- to assure the best possible service in behalf of each child by the worker and agency sharing responsibility through supervisory participation
- as an administrative function, to appraise whether the worker meets agency requirements and standards of performance
- in staff development, to promote the worker's growth on the job through individual and group teaching and through providing an appropriate channel for discussion and clarification of anxieties aroused by problems of children and parents

There should be an annual written evaluation of each worker by the supervisor, with provision for participation and reading by the worker. (9.71)

9.69 Inservice training of child care staff

An inservice training program for child care workers should be carried out by the agency to help them in their relationships with the children and with other child care practices and staff responsibilities in general.

The program should include:

- orientation courses for new staff members concerning agency purpose, objectives, resources, policies, services, and skills of child care
- training courses, including lectures and discussion, that encompass normal and deviant child behavior and development; professional child care practice; child care at various developmental levels; family relationships; variations in child-rearing patterns; types of emotional disturbance; effects of separation and deprivation; use and methods of discipline; group processes and their impact on individual children; confidentiality; ethnic and cultural awareness; use of materials, books, and records
- provision for attendance at courses, institutes, and conferences
- a library that includes child care, health, and sex education materials

9.70 Supervision of child care workers

Supervision should be provided as an essential element in the development of child care staff.

Child care workers should have regularly scheduled conferences with their supervisor.

Supervision should include opportunities for talking things over; for support and recognition; and for increasing self-awareness, self-confidence, and security in job performance.

Supervision should ensure that the purpose and objectives of the role that the child care worker is expected to carry out, as administratively defined, are generally understood and accepted.

The supervisor should have experience with children in group care, in addition to a master's degree. (9.41)

Consultation with other professional staff members is not a substitute for supervision.

The evaluation of the performance of the child care worker should take place in a planned conference with the supervisor at the end of the probationary period (three to six months following employment) and annually thereafter. (9.71)

Personnel Practices

Conditions of employment should be such that they will attract qualified staff, assure staff stability, reduce staff turnover, and be conducive to maintenance of a high quality of service and productivity.

9.71 Personnel policies and practices

In the voluntary agency, board and staff should participate in formulating personnel policies, which should be in writing, periodically reviewed and approved by the board. In the public agency, personnel administration, through a civil service or merit system, should provide an opportunity for advisory committees and staff to study its personnel policies and make recommendations.

A manual of personnel policies and practices, including job descriptions and all personnel forms used, should be maintained and available to applicants and employees at time of employment.

It should include:

• job descriptions; qualifications, duties, privileges, and extent of responsibilities of each position in the agency (9.34–9.66)
• salary ranges and provision for increments (9.72)

- hours of work, holidays, vacations, sick leave and other leaves (9.73–9.74)
- conditions of employment, tenure, promotion, and grievance procedure
- conditions and procedures for termination of employment
- time and method of staff evaluation
- employment benefits, including retirement plan, Social Security, hospitalization and other insurances

9.72 Salaries

Salaries should be adequate to attract staff with the necessary qualifications and preparation for the job.

Salaries should be set exclusive of maintenance so that staff members are able to live in the community outside the center.

Salaries should be commensurate with community standards, the education and experience of the applicant or employee, and equivalent to recommendations of national professional associations.

9.73 Working hours of child care staff

Child care staff members should have regularly scheduled hours of work, except for emergencies, which should allow time for outside activities and sufficient relaxation from the taxing demands of caring for and supervising a group of children.

Working excessive overtime may be a reflection of decreased effectiveness. Workers tend to press on with the task at hand. It may at times be necessary for the supervisor to point out when a worker needs to take a break.

Staff members should be encouraged to live in the community outside the residential facility.

All hours spent with the children, or in the interest of children and the living group, should be considered working hours.

No child care worker should regularly be with children more than 40 hours a week, exclusive of sleeping time.

Each staff member should have the equivalent of two full days off each week.

Daily schedules should allow for uninterrupted periods of relaxation; regular individual supervisory conferences; consultation with social workers and other staff members; required record keeping; attending staff conferences; and attending classes for child care staff when offered in the community.

Scheduling of shifts should allow for overlap to enable child care workers to exchange information about the children, so they will know what has happened while they were off duty and be able to deal consistently with each child and with the group.

It should be recognized that when child care staff members are overworked and are not provided with adequate relaxation periods, they are unable to meet the children's needs. Emotional and physical exhaustion frequently results in rejection of children, inability to give of oneself to emotionally deprived children, or low tolerance for hostility—behaviors that in turn are reflected in the behavior of the children.

9.74 Vacations of child care staff

All child care staff members should have a full month of paid vacation annually away from the agency.

9.75 Health examination for employees

All staff members working directly with the children, and those who may affect the health of the children through indirect contact by handling food, dishes, and other utensils, should have annual health examinations.

At the time of employment, it should be determined that any employee who will have direct contact with the children is in good physical health, on the basis of health history and a written statement from a physician regarding general health, specific illness or disability, and written reports of chest X-rays and other such tests as are indicated.

Employees who prepare or serve food should have, prior to employment, an examination in accordance with local public health regulations, although they may have little or no direct contact with children.

The agency should be prepared to pay for such examinations and for periodic reexaminations as prescribed by state or agency requirements.

Upon evidence of infectious disease or serious illness, an employee should stop work and not be allowed to return until his or her ability to function adequately on the job has been ascertained.

Recruitment and Training

9.76 Recruitment programs

To meet the need for well-suited child care staff, the agency should carry on an active program of recruitment and training.

Recruitment practices should be designed to attract suitable applicants with racial or ethnic backgrounds similar to those of the children served by the agency.

The agency should maintain close relationships with appropriate professional schools and should qualify as a setting for student training that offers opportunities for working with children and their families.

The agency should provide assistance to qualified staff members to attend appropriate educational programs.

Staff should be made available for vocational counseling and cooperation with college and high school officials to orient guidance counselors or students to child care and social work as vocations.

Development of training programs and college courses for child care workers should be actively promoted. (9.69)

Research

9.77 Responsibility for research

The agency should participate in joint research with other agencies and should carry on research to advance knowledge about children and about residential services.

In order that practice may be based on knowledge, the center has a responsibility to test assumptions and to determine the effects of the service through studies of decision making and through followup and longitudinal studies. The existence of a treatment plan for each child offers good ground for testing assumptions.

9.78 Program review and evaluation

Systematic fact gathering, such as data concerning reasons for placement, duration of stay in residential care, roles of various staff members, size of workloads, and costs should be carried on as a basis for evaluating the quality and quantity of service.

Evaluation can help the center decide whether to:

- continue or discontinue the program or some aspects of its service
- improve its practices and procedures
- add or drop particular program strategies and techniques
- institute similar programs elsewhere
- allocate resources among competing programs
- accept or reject a program approach or theory

9.79 Research staff

Research should be carried out with accepted research methodology under the direction of research personnel.

It should be recognized that research can be appropriately under-ᵗaken only when the researcher has sound professional qualifica-ions.

9.80 Protection of clients in research

The agency should take steps to assure that the privacy and the integrity of the children and their families are protected throughout all phases of its research program.

Appropriate safeguards to maintain confidentiality should be established. In followup studies that rely solely on agency records, where consent of a child or legal guardian would ordinarily not be sought, confidentiality should be respected.

The cooperation of a child who is old enough to understand the implications of confidentiality, or the cooperation of the legal guardian, should be voluntary. It should be made clear to them that the service is available regardless of their willingness to cooperate in any research program.

Interpretation to the Community

9.81 Interpretation program

Board and staff should carry on an active program of interpretation, education, and reporting to the community.

These activities are necessary:

- to account to the community for the responsibility delegated to the agency

- to enlist the support of an informed citizenry essential for adequate financing and promotion of effective, progressive agency services
- to establish a basis for working with other agencies and professions to improve the care of and services for children
- to bring about appropriate use of agency services and acceptance of them through informing members of the community who may need them
- to encourage appropriate and effective referrals for service from other community agencies and from key groups who often are sources of referral, such as other agencies, physicians, nurses, lawyers, the courts, clergy, teachers, and school principals

If the services of a public relations consultant are used, a thorough understanding of the agency's policy and program is essential. Participation in staff meetings or other agency activities offers a consultant the opportunity to understand all parts of the service.

Responsibility for Community Participation

Residential service is one of a complex of services. The agency providing it has a responsibility to identify unmet needs and to give leadership and stimulation for improvement of all child welfare services.

9.82 Planning and coordination of services

The agency should join with other residential facilities, community agencies, planning councils, denominational federations, public departments, and national agencies to plan, coordinate, and extend services for all children who require them, and to promote desirable standards of service. (9.1–9.5, 9.15–9.17)

Action should be taken to assure adequate services to all children according to their needs and to prevent gaps in services that are the consequence of lack of resources or restrictive eligibility requirements. (9.5)

For children whose needs cannot be met by existing agencies in the community, the agency should take part in efforts to develop the required services. (9.1)

Staff should be able to identify problems and gaps in service in the community, evident from the children and families served, and report their observations.

The agency board and staff should reassess the agency's services constantly, so that its program may be adapted to the changing needs of the children and the community.

The agency should cooperate with citizen and professional groups and with other social agencies concerned with strengthening family life and services to children and families.

The agency should know and use the resources of local, state, and national standard-setting and planning agencies, such as the Child Welfare League of America; and national authorities, such as the Children's Bureau in the U.S. Department of Health and Human Services, and in Canada, the provincial and federal governmental authorities.

The community relations function of the agency should be carried by the board of directors and staff, as well as by the executive.

10

COMMUNITY PLANNING AND ORGANIZATION OF A RESIDENTIAL CENTER

Community planning can provide leadership and assistance in coordinating residential services with other resources in the community, in adapting programs to the changing needs of children and their families, to other child welfare and community services, and to present-day standards. (10.9, 10.10)

Relation to Community Child Welfare Program

10.1 Basic health and welfare services

Community planning should seek to achieve a balanced pattern of community child welfare services, public and voluntary, so that the needs of all children can be appropriately met.

> To use residential services selectively for children, other services must be available. (0.3, 0.23)

> Services to children in their own homes are needed to strengthen and maintain families, to preserve for the child his or her own home, and to prevent the need for placement. These services include financial assistance, family service, homemaker service, day care, and day treatment services; protective service; public health services; medical and mental health services; recreational and

groupwork services; school social work, and juvenile and probation services.

Availability of foster family care with adequate social work services is a prerequisite for appropriate use of residential service. Adoption services should make it possible to consider adoption for children remaining in foster care for extended periods of time.

A range of group care services is needed to meet the needs of school-age and adolescent boys and girls; children with different types of personality disturbances requiring different treatment; and children with physical or mental handicaps precluding participation in normal family living. The range should include group homes, shelter care, detention care, residences serving delinquent children, and specialized treatment facilities.

10.2 Services for emotionally disturbed and developmentally disabled children

For children with severe disturbances in development and functioning, a range of treatment facilities under social agency and medical auspices, public and voluntary, should be available in the community so that services of a child welfare residential facility will be used appropriately for children who cannot be cared for and treated effectively in their own homes and families.

These services should include mental health centers, other outpatient psychiatric services, specialized foster family group homes, inpatient psychiatric services, specialized educational and health programs.

10.3 Services for children of minority groups

Residential services should be provided for children on the basis of their individual needs and problems, without restrictions based on race, color, ethnic origin, or their status as members of minority groups.

Services may be designed for a particular minority racial group provided that such services are made available to any other children who are able to use them.

10.4 Residential services under auspices of religious faiths

Residential services under auspices of religious faiths should be an integral part of the community child welfare program, and should be coordinated with each other and with other social services for children and families. (2.20, 3.51, 10.16)

The respective roles and contributions of sectarian and nonsectarian residential treatment services should be recognized.

The services of an agency under religious auspices may include practices consonant with the beliefs of its faith, in addition to those covered in the standards of the Child Welfare League of America.

When it has been determined in accordance with accepted social work practice that a child requires placement outside his or her home, full consideration should be given to the religious components in a child's life in deciding on the service, public or voluntary, that is providing care. The decision should be made after considering the wishes of the parent, the child, the availability of a facility under the auspices of the religious faith of the family, and the total plan for the care and treatment of the child.

If a public agency is not able to provide or assure regular care for the child, consideration can be given to the purchase of service from an agency that is related to the child's faith and is also able to meet adequately other needs of the child, provided that it meets the licensing requirements of the state. (10.8)

10.5 Interagency cooperation

Coordination of services and cooperative relationships should be assured through joint planning and agreements among agencies.

Focus on the changing needs of children requires interagency collaboration, conjoint, and/or consecutive services. Although a number of larger agencies have a relatively wide range of services available within their own organization, no single agency generally provides all the services that children and their families need.

Individual agencies providing child welfare services, regardless of auspice, must operate not in isolation, but as part of a larger system of services that have common goals and responsibilities. Each agency must be related to the other social institutions and service systems that have a commitment to children and offer services that implement their rights (income maintenance systems, schools, health and medical services, mental health services, family services, courts, recreational facilities, churches and synagogues, public housing, vocational services).

Relationship Between Public and Voluntary Agencies

Both public and voluntary residential services are essential to ensure coverage, full use of all available financial resources, leadership, and experimentation.

10.6 Respective responsibilities of public and voluntary agencies

Services of public and voluntary agencies should complement each other. Their respective responsibilities should be clarified, and the services should be fully and appropriately used through interagency cooperation and community planning.

Needs of children in the community, the stage of development of services, the sources and availability of funds and the structural pattern of services within the community should determine services to be given by public and voluntary agencies and the division of responsibility between them.

10.7 Public residential services

The public agency should make residential services available for all children for whom such services are appropriate, without restriction as to race, religion, economic status, or legal residence.

The public agency's responsibility is derived from the law.

The public agency should have the authority to provide services based on voluntary agreements with parents without court commitment, as well as to accept children through court action. Court action should not be required for public agencies to offer or purchase care for children.

10.8 Purchase of care

It is sound practice for a public agency to purchase, and a voluntary agency to sell, residential services that a particular child needs when the public agency cannot provide for individual children for whom it has accepted responsibility.

When public funds are paid to voluntary agencies, they should be given only in payment for care of individual children for whom the public agency has accepted responsibility. The public agency has a continuing responsibility to see that these children receive adequate care in accordance with their needs.

Public agencies should purchase services only from those agencies that meet standards of care established by the state department responsible for child welfare services. (9.4)

In purchasing service, public agencies should pay the full cost of service. (9.11)

Rates of payment should be commensurate with the nature and quality of services offered and should be on a per diem, per capita basis.

Written contractual agreements, mutually arrived at and clearly stating the respective responsibilities of the agencies involved, should regulate all purchase of care.

The voluntary agency should be free to maintain its own intake policies. (2.10, 9.15)

Community Provision for Residential Services

10.9 Role of planning body

The community planning body in the community and the state department that is responsible for child welfare services should provide leadership and resources for assessing the adequacy of the community's child welfare program; for coordinating, improving, and reorganizing existing services; for developing residential services and other services that are lacking; and for helping agencies individually and collectively to meet the needs of all children and families requiring services. (9.1)

10.10 Citizen participation

Community planning should be carried on through processes that fully involve citizen interest, participation, and action.

A continuing active partnership of professional and lay representatives of children and parents and other lay persons is required to achieve the objectives of planning. The professionals contribute knowledge about child welfare services, treatment of problems of children and their families, and technical skill in community organization; the citizens' role is primarily in social action, interpretation, and community relations. This participation not only furthers community planning, but can promote more adequate communication and financing of both voluntary and tax-supported services.

10.11 Financing of services

The planning body should advocate budgets for child welfare residential services and act as a guide in allocation of sufficient contributed funds from the community to obtain qualified personnel, to provide specialized services, and to maintain the well-being of children. It should also work actively for adequate public appropriations. (9.10, 9.11)

The planning organization should be informed about the financial needs and the particularities of residential services. (9.5, 9.36)

10.12 Legislation*

Community planning should be concerned with legislation affecting all child welfare services and should work for enactment or improvement of legislation pertaining to the licensing of child welfare residential services, the custody and guardianship of children, parental rights, adoption, public assistance, and other provisions to promote and safeguard the welfare and rights of children and parents. (2.17, 9.21–24, 10.13)

10.13 Licensing

Licensing should be required by law for all voluntary and sectarian agencies providing residential services for children, as well as for public agencies.

Licensing is a process and a community protection that not only assures maintenance of minimum standards, but also can provide leadership, stimulation, and improvement of service through consultation. (10.16)

Provisions for enforcement, including license denial or revocation for nonconformance, should be incorporated in legislation.

Licensing of residential programs should be done by qualified staff who have successful child welfare experience.

Licensing of child welfare residential services should be the responsibility of the state agency that is responsible for child welfare services, in consultation with health departments and other appropriate services.

---

* See *CWLA Statement on Child Advocacy*. Child Welfare League of America, 1981.

10.14 Direct service of the public agency

When the public agency has accepted responsibility for individual children, it should:
- make appropriate services available to them, either directly or by purchase or payments for such services provided by another agency
- assume responsibility for the payment for services to the extent that the parents are unable to do so
- assume legal custody or legal guardianship of children, vested by the court, when parental rights are temporarily abrogated or terminated
- take necessary action for appointment of a guardian of the person of children who do not have a parent to exercise effective guardianship
- carry continuing responsibility for seeing that the children and parents are receiving appropriate services in accordance with their needs

10.15 Role of the public agency responsible for child welfare services

The provincial, state, or local public department should give leadership in planning, establishing, and maintaining residential services throughout the state under both public and voluntary auspices.

The overall responsibilities of the public agency should include:
- provision of direct services for children and their parents
- provision for appeals, fair hearings, and grievances
- administrative supervision of its agencies providing direct services
- recommendations for approval of articles of incorporation of voluntary and proprietary agencies
- regulation of agencies
- evaluation and accountability
- leadership in program planning
- fact finding and reports
- staff development and training
- research and demonstration

10.16 Role of sectarian federations and agencies

Sectarian federations or agencies with a planning and leadership role in respect to the unique problems of children should carry out their functions within the framework of and in relation to overall community planning and activity.

10.17 Role of provincial, state, and national organizations

Agencies at the state, provincial, and national level should serve as resources in planning, consultation, coordination of residential services, research, standard setting, interpretation, organized social action, and promotion of interagency relationships.

State committees on children and youth, and state and regional associations for children's residential centers, should engage in study of the needs of the children and their families and work for greater understanding and improvement of services for them.

Federal, provincial, and national organizations should advocate for children's needs in general and for the needs of children of minorities in particular.

SELECTED REFERENCES

1. *A Policy Statement on Standards for Children's Residential Care Facilities.* Ontario, Canada: Children's Services Division, Ministry of Community and Social Services, 1980.
2. Adler, Jack. *The Child Care Worker 1975.* New York: Brunner/Mazel, 1976.
3. Aldgate, Jane. "Advantages of Residential Care." *Adoption and Fostering,* Vol. 92, No. 2, 1978.
4. Balbernie, Richard. *Residential Work with Children.* New York: Pergamon Press, Inc., 1966.
5. Barchi, Carl F. "A Community Reentry Model." *Child Welfare,* November 1977.
6. Beedell, Christopher. *Residential Life with Children.* New York: Humanities Press, 1970.
7. Becker, Jerome. *Critical Incidents in Child Care.* New York: Behavioral Publications, 1972.
8. _____. "Development of a Professional Identity for the Child Care Worker." *Child Welfare,* June 1975.
9. Berman, Samuel P. "A Report on a Child Welfare League of America Pilot Project to Train Child Care Workers." *Child Welfare,* March 1970.
10. Bremner, Robert H., editor. *Children and Youth in America—A Documentary History, Vol. 1: 1600–1865.* Cambridge, MA: Harvard University Press, 1970.
11. Brookwood Child Care. *The Family Residential Center: Experiment in Part-Time Parenthood.* New York: Brookwood Child Care, 1972.
12. Broten, Alton. *House Parents in Children's Institutions—A Discussion Guide.* Chapel Hill, NC: University of North Carolina Press, 1962.
13. Burmeister, Eva M. *Institutional Care for Children and Youth.* Madison, WI: The University of Wisconsin, 1966.
14. _____, and Kuhn, Roy. *Ten Case Studies: An Aid for Staff Development in Child Care Institutions.* Madison, WI: The University of Wisconsin, 1969.
15. Burt, Marvin R. "Final Results of the Nashville Comprehensive Emergency Services Project." *Child Welfare,* November 1976.
16. Chapman, Eldon. *Children for Auction.* New York: Vantage Press, 1978.
17. *Children's Residential Care Facilities: Proposed Standards and Guidelines.* Ontario, Canada: Children's Services Division, Ministry of Community and Social Services, 1978.
18. *Comprehensive Syllabus for a Child Welfare Training Program.* Washington, D.C.: U.S. Department of Health and Human Services, 1980.
19. Costin, Lela. *Child Welfare: Policies and Practice.* 2nd edition. New York: McGraw-Hill, 1979.

20. Dinnage, Rosemary, and Pringle, M.L. Killmer. *Residential Child Care: Facts and Fallacies.* New York: Humanities Press, 1967.

21. *Encyclopedia of Social Work.* 17th edition. Washington, D.C.: National Association of Social Workers, 1977.

22. Fanshel, David. "Parental Visiting of Children in Foster Care: Key to Discharge?" *Social Service Review,* December 1977.

23. Fanshel, David, and Shinn, Eugene B. *Children in Foster Care: A Longitudinal Investigation.* New York: Columbia University Press, 1978.

24. Fant, Raymond S., and Ross, Andrew L. "Supervision of Child Care Staff." *Child Welfare,* December 1979.

25. Folks, Homer. *The Care of Destitute, Neglected and Delinquent Children.* New York: The Macmillan Company, 1911.

26. Group Child Care Consultant Services. *The Basic Course for Residential Child Care Workers.* Chapel Hill, NC: University of North Carolina, 1978.

27. Gula, Martin. *Child-Caring Institutions.* Washington, D.C.: U.S. Government Printing Office, 1958.

28. Hechler, Jacob. "Social Controls in Institutional Treatment." *Social Work,* April 1956.

29. Jaffe, E.D. "The Impact of Experimental Services on Dependent Children Referred for Institutional Care." *Social Work Today,* May 1970.

30. Jenkins, Shirley, and Sauber, Mignon. *Paths to Child Placement: Family Situations Prior to Foster Care.* New York: Department of Welfare and the Community Council of Greater New York, 1966.

31. _____, and Norman, Elaine. *Filial Deprivation and Foster Care.* New York: Columbia University Press, 1972.

32. _____. *Beyond Placement:* *Mothers View Foster Care.* New York: Columbia University Press, 1975.

33. Kadushin, Alfred. *Child Welfare Services.* 3rd edition. New York: Macmillan Publishing Co., 1980 (chapter 11, pg. 583–630).

34. Kahn, Alfred. *When Children Must Be Committed.* New York: Citizens' Committee for Children of New York, 1960.

35. Kamerman, Sheila B., and Kahn, Alfred S. *Social Services in the United States—Policies and Programs.* Philadelphia, PA: Temple University Press, 1976.

36. Keith-Lucas, Alan, and Sanford, Clifford W. *Group Child Care as a Family Service.* Chapel Hill, NC: University of North Carolina Press, 1977.

37. Klein, Alan F. *The Professional Child Care Worker—A Guide to Skills, Knowledge, Techniques and Attitudes.* New York: Association Press, 1975.

38. Konopka, Gisela. *Group Work in the Institution.* Revised edition. New York: Association Press, 1970.

39. _____. "What Houseparents Should Know," in *Children in Care.* R.J.N. Tod, editor. London, England: Longman Group Ltd., 1968.

40. Krause, Kenneth. "Authoritarianism, Dogmatism and Coercion in Child Caring Institutions: A Study of Staff Attitudes." *Child Welfare,* January 1974.

41. Lambert, Paul. *The ABC's of Child Care Work in a Residential Setting.* New York: Child Welfare League of America, 1977.

42. _____. "Memo to Child Care Workers: Notes on the Management of Sex and Stealing." *Child Welfare,* May 1976.

43. Lutheran Council in the U.S.A. "A Perspective on Residential Child Care Programs." *Child Welfare,* January 1972.

44. Maas, Henry, and Engler, Richard. *Children in Need of Care.* New

York: Columbia University Press, 1959.

45. Martin, Lawrence; Pozdnjakoff, Ija; and Wilding, Joyce. "The Use of Residential Care." *Child Welfare*, April 1976.

46. Mayer, Margaret. "Family Ties and the Institutional Child." *Children*, November–December 1969.

47. Mayer, Morris F.; Richman, Leon H.; and Balcerzak, Edwin A. *Group Care of Children: Crossroads and Transitions*. New York: Child Welfare League of America, 1977.

48. _____, *A Guide for Child Care Workers*. New York: Child Welfare League of America, 1958.

49. _____, *Supervision of Houseparents*. New York: Child Welfare League of America, 1953.

50. _____. "Training for Child Care Work: A Report on a National Conference." *Child Welfare*, November 1969.

51. Miller, Margaret D. "Improving Standards for Child Care Institutions: A Study in Procedure." *Child Welfare*, April 1974.

52. Moyles, William E., and Wolins, Martin. "Group Care and Intellectual Development." *Developmental Psychology*, Vol. 4, No. 3, 1971.

53. Pappenfort, Donnell, et al. *A Census of Children's Residential Institutions in the U.S., Puerto Rico and the Virgin Islands: 1966. Vol. 1: Seven Types of Institutions*. Chicago: University of Chicago School of Social Service Administration, 1970.

54. _____. *A Census of Children's Residential Institutions in the U.S., Puerto Rico and the Virgin Islands: 1966. Vol. 2: Institutions for Dependent and Neglected Children*. Chicago: University of Chicago School of Social Service Administration, 1970.

55. Pappenfort, Donnell, and Kilpatrick, Dee M. "Child Caring Institutions 1966: Selected Findings from the First National Survey of Children's Residential Institutions." *Social Service Review*, December 1969.

56. Pappenfort, Donnell M.; Kilpatrick, Dee M.; and Roberts, Robert W., editors. *Child Caring: Social Policy and the Institution*. Chicago: Aldine Publishing Company, 1973.

57. Phillips, Michael H.; Shyne, Ann W.; Sherman, Edmund A.; and Haring, Barbara L. *Factors Associated with Placement Decisions in Child Welfare*. New York: Child Welfare League of America, 1971.

58. Piliavin, Irving. "Conflict Between Cottage Parents and Caseworkers." *Social Service Review*, March 1963.

59. Prosser, Hilary. *Perspective on Residential Child Care: An Annotated Bibliography*. New York: Humanities Press, 1976.

60. Provence, Sally. *Guide for the Care of Infants in Groups*. New York: Child Welfare League of America, 1967.

61. Reichertz, Diane. *Residential Care: The Impact of Institutional Policies, Structures and Staff on Resident Children*. Montreal, Canada: School of Social Work, McGill University, 1978.

62. *Residential Child Care Guidebook*. Trenton, N.J.: The Interstate Consortium on Residential Child Care, Department of Human Services, 1980.

63. Rozentals, Vaira. "Professionalizing the Child Care Worker." *Child Welfare*, November 1974.

64. Rutter, Michael. *Maternal Deprivation Reassessed*. Maryland: Penguin Books. 1981.

65. Schulze, Susanne. *Creative Group Living in Children's Institutions*. New York: Association Press, 1951.

66. Seidl, Frederick. "Community-Oriented Residential Care: The State of the Art." *Child Care Quarterly*, Fall 1974.

67. Sherman, Edmund A; Neuman, Renee; and Shyne, Ann W. *Children Adrift in Foster Care: A Study of Alternative Approaches.* New York: Child Welfare League of America, 1973.

68. Shulman, Rena. "Examples of Adolescent Group Homes in Alliance with Larger Institutions." *Child Welfare,* May 1975.

69. Special Report. "A Guide for Consultation in Training Child Care Aides." *Child Welfare,* July 1972.

70. *Standards for Children's Residential Care Facilities.* Ontario, Canada: Children's Services Division, Ministry of Community and Social Services, 1980.

71. Steele, Carolyn I. "Sex Role Identity of Adolescent Girls in Foster Homes and Institutions." *Child Welfare,* June 1972.

72. Stevens, George T., and Mueller, Carl. "A Child Care Career Model." *Child Welfare,* May 1976.

73. Thomas, George. *A Community-Oriented Evaluation of the Effectiveness of Child Caring Institutions.* Final Report to the Office of Child Development, HEW Project No. OCD-CB 106. Athens, GA: Regional Institute of Social Welfare Research, 1975.

74. Tizard, Jack: Sinclair, Ian; and Clarke, R.V.G, editors. *Varieties of Residential Experience.* London, England: Routledge and Kegan Paul, 1975.

75. Tod, Robert J.N. *Children in Care.* London, England: Longmans, Green and Company, 1968.

76. Toigo, Romulo. "Child Care Manpower Development: A Literature Review." *Child Care Quarterly,* Spring 1975.

77. Trasler, Gordon. *In Place of Parents.* London, England: Kegan Paul, Trench, Trubner and Co., 1960.

78. United States Office of Comptroller General. *Children in Foster Care Institutions—Steps Government Can Take to Improve Their Care.* Washington, D.C.: U.S. Government Printing Office, 1977.

79. Whittaker, James K. "The Changing Character of Residential Child Care: An Ecological Perspective." *Social Service Review,* March 1978.

80. Witmer, Helen, and Gershenson, Charles P. *On Rearing Infants and Young Children in Institutions.* Children's Bureau Research Reports. No. 1. Washington, D.C.: U.S. Government Printing Office, 1968.

81. Wolins, Martin, editor. *Successful Group Care: Exploration in the Powerful Environment.* Chicago: Aldine Publishing Company, 1974.

82. _____. "Group Care: Friend or Foe." *Social Work,* January 1969.

83. Wolins, Martin and Piliavin, Irving. *Institution or Foster Family: A Century of Debate.* New York: Child Welfare League of America, 1964.

84. _____. "Young Children in Institutions—Some Additional Evidence." *Developmental Psychology,* Vol. 2, No. 1, 1969.

INDEX

Communications system, 8.32
Community activities, 3.54
Community child welfare program, agency's relation to, 10.1–10.5
Community participation, responsibility for, 9.82
Community provision for residential services: planning body, 10.9; citizen participation, 10.10; financing of services, 10.11; legislation, 10.12; licensing, 10.13; direct service of public agency, 10.14; role of public agency, 10.15; role of sectarian federations and agencies, 10.16; role of provincial, state, and national organizations, 10.17
Confidentiality of records, 9.31, 9.80
Contract for care, between parents and agency, 2.23
Cottage parents, see Child care staff
Counselors, see Child care staff
Court, referrals by, 2.3
Cultural activities, provision for, 8.19
Custody, see Legal custody

D

Decision to accept child, 2.10
Dental care, 3.43, 9.59
Disaster planning, 8.41
Discipline, 3.25; responsibility for, 5.6
Doctor, see Physician

E

Education in residential care, responsibility for, 4.1–4.2
Education plan, 4.3–4.6
Educational administrator, 4.14
Educational program, 4.7–4.9
Emergency placement, 2.4
Executive director: residence of, 8.18; responsibilities of, 9.36; qualifications of, 9.37; assistants to, 9.38

F

Family, preservation of, 0.21
Family life, 0.20
Family therapy, 6.8
Fire prevention and detection, 8.39–8.40
Food, 3.17, 9.47
Foster family care, 0.22

G

Group activity and discussion groups, 7.6
Group living: minimizing hazards in, 0.11; cottage type, 0.15; program for, 3.1–3.2; responsibility for, 3.3; size of, 3.4; staff coverage, 3.5; as a treatment method, 3.11; personal care, 3.14; controls, 3.15; daily routines, 3.16
Group living experiences, 0.4; providing, 5.5
Group meeting, 5.5
Group parents, see Child care staff
Group punishment, 3.27
Grouping, 3.2–3.4; staff coverage in, 3.5; by age, 3.6
Groupwork: use of, 7.1; with children, 7.6; with parents, 7.7
Groupwork records, 7.8
Groupworker: skills of, 7.1; responsibilities of, 7.2–7.11; relationships with other staff members, 7.12–7.13
Guardianship, 9.23

H

Health education, 3.35
Health examination, of employees, 9.75
Health program, responsibility for, 3.29–3.30
Health records, 3.41
Health services, 3.29–3.43
Heating system, 8.38
Holidays, 3.49
Hospitalization, 3.40
House parents, see Child care staff
Housekeeping, 5.9; staff, 9.48

I

Immunization, 3.33
Indian children, as special concern, 0.2
Individual, value of, 0.19
Individualization, of child, 5.3
Intake study, 2.5–2.9; role of social worker in, 6.3
Interagency cooperation, 10.5
Interpretation, to community, 9.81
Interviews: with child, 6.9; with parents, 6.11

K

Kitchen, furnishings and equipment, 8.23

L

Laundry, furnishings and equipment, 8.24
Legal custody, 9.22. *See also* Guardianship
Legal status, of child, 9.25
Leisure and play equipment, 8.35
Licensing, 10.13
Living group, 3.2–3.9. *See also* Activity group; Group living; Treatment group
Living units: layout of, 8.6–8.7, 8.10–8.18; furnishings and equipment of, 8.8–8.10, 8.12–8.16

M

Maintenance staff, 9.48
Medical and dental care, responsibility for, 2.19
Medical care, 3.37
Medical facilities, 8.29
Medical staff, 9.58
Medication, 3.38
Mental health services, 3.44–3.46
Misbehavior, 3.26

N

Newcomer groups, 7.6
Nurse, 0.5, 9.60
Nursing service, 3.42
Nutritionist, 3.17, 9.47

O

Office staff, 9.49
Outdoor play area, 8.20

P

Parent discussion groups, 7.7
Parental rights, protection of, 2.18
Parents: services for, 2.16; participation in placement, 2.17; responsibility for support of child, 2.20; social work with, 6.11; contact between children and, 2.22; child care staff and, 5.10; and preparation for child's discharge, 6.14; after discharge, 6.15
Payment of children for work, 3.24
Peer groups, 0.8
Personal hygiene, 3.19
Personal possessions, 3.21
Personnel policies and practices, 9.71–9.76
Physical examination, 3.31; frequency of, 3.34
Physician, 0.5, 9.58
Placement: preparation for, 2.12; services for child in, 2.13–2.15; services for parents in, 2.16–2.23; role of social worker in, 6.6–6.7
Planning a residential facility, 8.1–8.5. *See also* Residential center, organization of
Preparation for discharge groups, 7.6
Program coordinator, 9.39
Programming for group living, 3.1–3.2; daily living experiences, 3.14–3.28
Psychiatrist, 0.5, 3.44, 9.61
Psychologist, 0.5, 3.45, 9.62
Public and voluntary agencies, relationship between, 10.6–10.8
Punishment, 3.27

Q

Quarterly evaluation, 2.15

R

Recreation, 3.47–3.50; provision for, 8.19
Recreation workers, 7.10, 7.13, 9.46
Referrals, 2.1, 2.3; responsibility of agency in, 2.2; to another agency, 2.11; role of social worker in, 6.4
Religion, 3.51–3.53
Religious consultant, 3.52, 9.65
Relinquishment, 6.13
Research, 9.77–9.80
Residential care: common elements in, 0.2; selective use of, 0.3; distinctive values of, 0.4–0.11, 0.22
Residential care center: as a child welfare service, 0.1, 1.1–1.10, 2.1–2.26;

planning and programming, 0.5; routine and controls, 0.7; interpersonal relationships in, 0.9; changing role of, 0.12; group relations in, 0.16; social work in, 0.17; child care work in, 0.18; optimal size of, 3.12; school, 4.10–4.17; planning for, 8.1–8.5; medical facilities in, 8.29; communications in, 9.19; procedures for appeal, 9.20; staffing, 9.32–9.65

Residential care facility: building plans, 8.1; location, 8.2; grounds, 8.3; maintenance, 8.4; access, 8.5; undertaking a building program for handicapped, 8.5; living units, 8.6–8.18; central facilities, 8.19–8.22; central services, 8.23–8.25; administrative offices, 8.26–8.28; medical facilities in, 8.29; staff offices, 8.30–8.31; communication system, 8.32; furnishings and equipment, 8.34–8.36; sanitation and safety, 8.37–8.41

Residential center, organization of: auspices, 9.1; authorization, 9.2; incorporation, 9.3; licensing, 9.4; board of directors, 9.5–9.7; board committees, 9.8–9.9; budget, 9.10; costs of service, 9.11; sources of support, 9.12; audit, 9.13; policies and procedures, 9.14–9.15; agency manual, 9.16; departmentalization and decentralization, 9.17

Residential center school, *see* Center school

Residential services: basic assumptions in providing, 0.19–0.22; purpose of, 1.1; related to needs of children, 1.4; core components in, 1.5; total of, 1.6; integration of, 1.8, 9.18

Rights: of child, 1.10; of parents, 2.18

S

Safety, requirements for: 3.13; 8.37; heating system, 8.38; fire prevention, 8.39; fire protection, 8.40; disaster plans, 8.41

Sanitation, requirements for, 8.37

School: attendance, 4.2; records, 4.17

School and school rooms, planning of, 8.21

Sex education, 3.36

Sickness, 3.39

Sleep, 3.18

Social agency, legal responsibilities of: assumption of responsibility for children, 9.21; legal custody, 9.22; guardianship, 9.23; and termination of parental rights, 9.24; and legal status of child, 9.25; confidentiality of records, 9.31, 9.80

Social work: primary responsibility of, 0.1; use of, 6.1; with child, 6.5–6.10; with parents, 6.11–6.15

Social work staff: director, 9.50; supervisor, 9.51; graduate social workers, 9.52; social groupworker, 9.53; social workers, 9.54; specialists and consultants, 9.56–9.65

Social worker, 0.5, 0.10, 0.16, 3.46, 9.54; responsibilities of, 6.2–6.4; relationship to child, 6.5; treatment of problems of child, 6.8; working with parents, 6.11–6.12; and case records, 6.16–6.17; relationship with groupworker, 7.12; workload of, 9.55

Specialists and consultants: basis for employment, 9.56; qualifications, 9.57

Staff development program, 9.67

Statistics, reporting, and records, 9.27–9.31

Substitute care, selection of, 0.22

Swimming pool, 8.35

T

Teachers, 0.5, 9.63; training program for, 4.15

Team approach, 1.9

Termination of parental rights, 9.24

Termination of service, 2.24–2.25; aftercare, 2.26; preparation for, 6.10

Transportation, 8.36

Treatment, differences in concepts of, 0.13–0.14

Treatment group, 3.11, 7.6. *See also* Activity group; Living group

Treatment plan, 1.7

Tutoring, 3.28, 4.9

U

Utility equipment, general, 8.25

V

Vocational counseling and training, 4.8
Volunteer group leaders, 7.11

Volunteers: use of, 3.55; selection and training of, 9.66

W

Work assignments, 3.23

St. Scholastica Library
Duluth, Minnesota 55811